FRIENDS
OF THUNDER

Folktales of the Oklahoma Cherokees

FRIENDS OF THUNDER

Folktales of the Oklahoma Cherokees

JACK F. KILPATRICK
ANNA G. KILPATRICK

Foreword by
ROBERT J. CONLEY

UNIVERSITY OF OKLAHOMA PRESS • NORMAN AND LONDON

By Jack F. Kilpatrick and Anna G. Kilpatrick

Friends of Thunder: Folktales of the Oklahoma Cherokees (Dallas, 1964)
The Shadow of Sequoyah: Social Documents of the Cherokees, 1862–1964 (Norman, 1965)
Walk in Your Soul: Love Incantations of the Oklahoma Cherokees (Dallas, 1965)
Run Toward the Nightland: Magic of the Oklahoma Cherokees (Dallas, 1967)
New Echota Letters: Contributions of Samuel A. Worcester to the Cherokee Phoenix (Dallas, 1968)

Library of Congress Cataloging-in-Publication Data
Kilpatrick, Jack Frederick.
  Friends of thunder : folktales of the Oklahoma Cherokees / Jack F. Kilpatrick,
Anna G. Kilpatrick ; foreword by Robert J. Conley.
    p. cm.
  Originally published: Dallas : Southern Methodist University Press, ©1964.
  Includes bibliographical references.
  ISBN 0-8061-2722-8 (alk. paper)
    1. Cherokee Indians—Folklore. 2. Cherokee mythology. 3. Tales—Okla-
homa. I. Kilpatrick, Anna Gritts. II. Title.
E99.C5K48 1994
398.2'089'975—dc20   94-34098
                                                                CIP

Published by the University of Oklahoma Press, Norman, Publishing Division of the
University. Copyright ©1964 by Southern Methodist University Press, transferred in
1994 to the University of Oklahoma Press. Foreword by Robert J. Conley copyright
©1995 by the University of Oklahoma Press. All rights reserved. Manufactured in the
U.S.A. First printing of the University of Oklahoma Press edition, 1995.

1 2 3 4 5 6 7 8 9 10

CONTENTS

TALES OF MONSTERS

THE LITTLE PEOPLE

TSEG'SGIN' STORIES

TALES OF HUMOR

MISCELLANEOUS STORIES

HISTORICAL SKETCHES

FOREWORD

If the work of the Cherokee husband and wife team of Jack Frederick and Anna Gritts Kilpatrick (gathering, translating, commenting on and publishing traditional Cherokee texts) has any rival at all, it is that done by James Mooney just before the turn of the century for the now defunct Bureau of American Ethnology.

Mooney's work is monumental: *Myths of the Cherokee*, *Sacred Formulas of the Cherokee*, and *The Swimmer Manuscript* (completed by Frans Olbrechts after Mooney's death). Yet while Mooney's work is invaluable to Cherokee scholars (or scholars of things Cherokee), it has its shortcomings. Mooney was an outsider looking in on Cherokee culture. A nineteenth-century ethnologist, he approached his subject with the paternalistic skepticism typical of his contemporary colleagues.

For example, Mooney writes in the introduction to *Sacred Formulas of the Cherokee*, "It is absurd to suppose that the savage, a child in intellect, has reached a higher development in any branch of science than has been attained by the civilized man, the product of long ages of intellectual growth." In *Myths of the Cherokee*, he writes this: "The unpleasant smell of the groundhog's head was given it by the other animals to punish an insulting remark made by him in council. The story is a vulgar one, without wit enough to make it worth recording." (No. 32.)

The Kilpatricks' books are substantially different from Mooney's. Jack, a mixed-blood Cherokee composer and musicologist, and his wife Anna, a full-blood Cherokee native speaker, found beauty in the language, marveled at Cherokee poetic structures and devices, and delighted in Cherokee cultural traditions revealed in the texts they collected, studied, and enjoyed.

It is precisely this enjoyment that so enriches their work, for when they prepared their manuscripts for publication, they did so with the clear intention of passing on to their readers that feeling of joy, delight, and wonder. Yet they did not sacrifice or ignore the rules of sound scholarship, providing a plethora of footnotes and citations for those readers who care to browse in academic pastures. With the Kilpatricks' Cherokee books, then, the reader gets the best of both worlds—a vivid illustration of what the Kilpatricks themselves termed, in their preface to *Friends of Thunder,* "the amazing ability of the Cherokees to maintain an equilibrium between two opposing worlds of thought."

The tales collected and presented in this volume are divided into nine topics: Bird Stories, Animal Stories, Uk'ten' Stories, Tales of Monsters, The Little People, Tseg'sgin' Stories, Tales of Humor, Miscellaneous Stories, and Historical Sketches. Music accompanies the lyrics when a song is incorporated into the story. (This element is lacking in Mooney's collection, a fact bemoaned by the Kilpatricks.)

The Bird and Animal stories are set in the ancient time, when animals all could converse with one another. These stories almost always do one of two things: they tell us how something came to be the way it is today "Why the Possum's Tail Is Bare"), or they supply a lesson for behavior or an exercise in good sense. First of all, though, they're just good, entertaining tales.

Uk'ten' tales and other monster tales from the Cherokee past are always fascinating, and it is a great pleasure to find new (i.e., previously unpublished) stories as well as old retold in this book. Regarding the Tseg'sgin' stories, I know of no place other than this collection where one can find them in print. Their central character, who is "unlovable, reprehensible, [and] basically dull," may be the Devil or Andrew Jackson—or both.

Many of these stories are ancient but over the years have incorporated modern elements. "The Rabbit Dupes the Wolf," for example, begins, "Now somewhere the Rabbit and the Wolf had killed a cow." The original tale could not have included a cow, because the Cherokees did not know of cows until the Spaniards brought them to this continent. Thus, the Cherokee word for *cow* is *wahka,* from the Spanish *vaca.* Similarly, in "The Hunter and the Uk'ten'," the hunter has a gun. The tales not only survive; they adapt.

Alternatively, some of the Kilpatricks' stories cannot be more than one-hundred years old. Legends developed from the lives of people both prominent and notorious and presented here as Historical Sketches, they include relatively modern myths about the Civil War, Sequoyah, and Cherokee Bill.

Friends of Thunder is rounded out beautifully with discussion about the storytellers themselves, including some actual dialogue between the Kilpatricks and various informants. Particularly intriguing is an exchange between a brother and sister, seventy-nine and eighty-two years old respectively, who accuse each other of witchcraft.

There is more to be learned from one book of the Kilpatricks than from several volumes of anthropological and ethnological gatherings and analyses. What's more, the learning is just plain fun.

ROBERT J. CONLEY

Tahlequah, Oklahoma
June 1994

PREFACE

What Herman F. C. ten Kate wrote toward the end of the last century was perceptive, but somewhat premature: ". . . with the full blood Cherokees, these legends and traditions [in his *Legends of the Cherokees*] will pass away forever, unless they are saved from oblivion by some lover of Indian folk-lore; and soon, or it will be too late." For with something approaching ease, some three-quarters of a century later in the summer of 1961, we amassed the material contained in this book.

Dr. ten Kate had not taken into account the amazing ability of the Cherokees to maintain an equilibrium between two opposing worlds of thought. Even today the Cherokee businessman, on the way to his country club, can be wrapped in deep speculation as to the exact height of the slant-eyed giant, Tsuhl'gûl', or the correct dosage of a decoction of *dalôn'ust'* for a recalcitrant kidney. Behind the television set in the cabin of his fellow tribesman lurk the Little People, and the Bible and Thunder share Cherokee reverence.

We wish to encore the ten Kate jeremiad, however, in view of the apparently incurable necrosis in the medium that has been responsible for preserving traditional thought, the language. The conservators of archival deposits of manuscript material in Cherokee must surely be increasingly aware that they but keep watch over the dead; and with a constantly increasing proportion of each new generation unable to speak the language, it is evident that collecting expeditions such as ours face a bleak future.

We tape-recorded our material in a variety of physical circumstances, none of which, very possibly, was considered ideal either by recorder or recorded. We taped from the tail of a pickup truck in the middle of a hill-country road ringing with the call of birds and the plash of a nearby stream; we recorded against the opposition of romping and querulous children, of barking dogs and clucking fowls, and the clatter of a hay baler.

And we were reminded again and again that there is no other way to the soul of our reserved but kindly people but through consanguinity. "What was your mother's name?" was the almost inevitable counter to any attempt to question them. The establishment of ties by blood immediately created a rapport that dissolved all barriers.

In our translation we have endeavored to present, insofar as possible, the exact words of the speaker; and if this statement or that plays fast and loose with English grammar, the reader may derive what comfort he can from the fact that the original Cherokee suffered from a similar defect. For the most part what we have excised was irrelevant or tending to jeopardize the anonymity of the speaker. Repetitions and redundancies are preserved for the purpose of maintaining the distinctive flavor of the language.

Words or phrases necessary to complete a meaning are enclosed in square brackets. Everything said in English is italicized.

While Cherokee must surely be one of the supreme accomplishments of man as a means for oral transference of thought, in reality no one has ever succeeded in capturing it in writing. With all of its weaknesses, the Sequoyah syllabary is still probably the most successful attempt; but since it requires special type faces, it could not be used. We decided to employ for words in Cherokee a simple system of orthography based upon the Sequoyah syllabic values. Its only merit is simplicity, we admit.

We acknowledge with deepest gratitude that this study was made possible by fellowships from the Southern Methodist University Graduate Council of the Humanities. We wish to express especial thanks to Dean Claude C. Albritton and Professor Albert C. Outler of that body for invaluable advice and encouragement.

JACK F. KILPATRICK
ANNA G. KILPATRICK

Dallas, Texas
March 1, 1964

CONTRIBUTORS

(Ages are given as of the date of recording)

Ahama—age, late 70's; male, married; retired farmer and minor public official; Christian, Baptist; English, poor.

Anisgay'dih'—age, 30; male, married; Korean War veteran, employee of aircraft accessory factory, Wichita, Kans.; Christian, Baptist; English, good.

Asudi—age, 92; male, married, farmer; Christian, probably Baptist; English, fair.

Dadayi—age, about 70; female, married; probably Christian, Baptist; English, poor.

Dalala (M.)—age, 70; male, married; World War I veteran, stockman; Christian, Baptist; English, fair.

Dalala (N.)—age, 79; male, widower; retired farmer [?]; Christian, Baptist; English, almost none. [Died 1963.]

Diyôhli—age, about 60; male, married; farmer; Christian, Methodist; English, good. Wife is white woman.

Dôi—age, about 76; male, married; World War I veteran, retired farmer [?]; Christian, probably Baptist; English, fair. [Died 1964.]

Ganahw'sôsg'—age, 68; male, married; World War I veteran, retired farmer, logger; Christian; Baptist; English, almost none.

Gahnô—age, 82; female, widow; farm-wife; probably non-Christian; English, poor. [Died 1963.]

Galûts'—age, 67; male, married; farmer; probably Christian, Baptist; English, fair.

Gatey'—age, late 70's; female, married; retired farm-wife; Christian, Baptist; English, poor.

Sgequa—age, 77; male, married, retired farmer; probably Christian, Methodist; English, fair. Wife is white woman.

Siquanid'—age, about 50; male, married; Baptist minister; English, fair.

Tlutlu—age, late 70's; male, widower; retired railroad employee; Christian, Baptist; English, poor. [Died 1961.]

Tsiwôn'—age, 68; female, married; housewife; Christian, Baptist; English, fair.

Yan'sa—age, 81; male, married; farmer; Christian, Baptist; English, almost none.

THE STORYTELLERS

ᎤᎾᏓᏡᎦᏃ ᎤᎧᏲᎢᎯᏴᏗ ᏗᏂᏓ

ᏣᏁᏆᎵᏆᏯᎢ ᏗᎠᎥᏣ ᎨᏅᏂ

"It is amazing, the number of things they used to tell . . ."

THE STORYTELLERS

THE STORYTELLERS ON STORYTELLING

There is little evidence to indicate that the Oklahoma Cherokees of today sanction any individuals, or class of individuals, as repositories for oral tradition—excepting, of course, that material relative to primitive religion and medicine. In the narrating of an animal myth, for instance, the didahnûwisg" *enjoys no advantage through prerogative or skill over the deacon; in fact, the latter would probably hold the edge over the former, with his more outgoing personality and more extensive experience in public speaking.*

Storytelling would appear to be largely a matter of personal interest, individual turn of mind. There are those Cherokees who hugely relish a good tale and become expansive in the telling of it; there are those who fumble self-consciously through what they must regard as something of a chore. And there are those, in the majority, who make good listeners, but would just as soon announce their intention of running for Congress as attempt the spinning of a yarn.

In the Cherokee Hills there is a general feeling that age does not necessarily beget better storytelling, but merely greater opportunity for drinking at the fount of the past. In other words, one is talented, or one is not.

And rare is the narrator who does not express or imply at some juncture in one's conversation with him a painful sense of desuetude in the exercise of his skill. He nostalgically reaches back after the magic of long nights spent around the winter fireplace, sitting at the feet of long-dead masters of verbal mood-making, whose names, garlanded with a respectful tsigesû' *(used to be: "late"), roll lovingly over his tongue.*

3

Likely as not he harbors a dark suspicion that the art of story-telling among the Cherokees has fallen upon evil, perhaps final, days—a point of view based upon the hard realities of, say, a son who has assumed permanent residence in Chicago, a grandson who can neither speak nor understand a single word of Cherokee.

One storyteller listening to the taped voice of another is capable of giving way to unbounded admiration or to deprecation engendered by jealousy or a conviction of superiority. Depending upon the status of the taped speaker, one is apt to hear critiques patterned upon the following: "He doesn't tell it right," or "He's a good storyteller, but I heard this one a little differently."

All appear to strive painfully for accuracy according to their lights. All exude a willingness to do their best. But over and above this is a prideful eagerness, to the authors infinitely moving, to share what they consider to be something peculiarly Cherokeean with those who, like themselves, are Cherokees by blood, birth, and upbringing.

"The Things They Told Long Ago"

The things they told long ago are very interesting to hear. It is almost impossible to remember it [what was told] all. It seems that one can remember only a small amount of it. When people can remember all of it, they can tell very interesting things.

Many people do not tell the stories right: they get them all mixed up. That is the reason why these stories sometimes vary. Some people know more of the stories, some less.

Siquanid'

"When I Am Sitting Here Alone"

It is amazing, the number of things they used to tell in comparison to what they tell today. It is very difficult to find someone who can tell these stories, someone who can recall them.

When I am sitting here alone, I can remember most of it [what I once knew], but when I have to do it [tell stories] very quickly [on short notice], I can't remember. It is only when I can sit down and think a long time that I can do it. That's the way it is.

There are some things I do remember of the events of long ago that they told about, these events that they passed down. "Everything is just as God planned. He made everything the way it is, and He planned the way all things should live"—that's what they talked about. And they also included comical things in their talks. In their conversations they would come to these jokes and then go back to more serious things. Then they would continue and say, "This is what he did; this is what he'll do; this is what he did." They would ask, "Who started that?" There was always someone who knew, and he would answer instantly.

That's the way you heard things, and if you didn't pay any attention, you wouldn't know anything. If you had paid attention, you would know.

Asudi

BIRD STORIES

ᎣᏂ ᏓᏆ ᏐᏁᏉᎠ ᎨᏒ ᎦᏌᏫ

"All the young women loved the Hummingbird."

BIRD STORIES

The relatively sparse material that we obtained on birds cannot be accepted as other than the operation of chance: we simply interviewed those who knew, or wanted to tell, few bird stories. There is ample evidence to indicate the existence in the last century of a multitude of avian myths; there is some evidence to support the hypothesis that a good many still survive.

The most surprising hiatus in our collection is the absence of owl stories; for the uguku *(hoot owl) and the* wahuhi *(screech owl) figure largely in affairs Cherokeean. But since both of these nocturnal birds are intimately associated with the occult, we may have been doing our delving in a thought-stratum essentially unfriendly to owls.*

Study in Fire, Gold, and Ice

The Redbird (*totsuhwa*) and the Yellow Mockingbird *(huhu)* are assigned roles in several of the most beautiful of the myths of the Eastern Cherokees. They are starred together in this fragile and evanescent mythic idyl of the Western Cherokees. It would appear never before to have been collected.

It was recorded in the Natchez country in the front yard of a cabin set beside a singing wilderness of laden blackberry bushes in a delicious cove not far from the swift Illinois River which here, below Tenkiller Lake, is much frequented by waterfowl.

The Yellow Mockingbird Desires To See Ice
The Redbird and the Yellow Mockingbird:
The Yellow Mockingbird had never seen ice. The Redbird said

9

to him, "I'll save you some, and when you return, you must examine it."

"All right," said he [the Yellow Mockingbird], and went south.

When winter came, ice was saved for the Yellow Mockingbird. When the Yellow Mockingbird returned in the spring, he said, "Where is the ice?"

"Well, just two days ago it melted," he was told—Tsisqua *told the Redbird.*[1]

That's all.

Tlutlu

Slow but Sure: Or, All Is Not Gold That Glisters

There is a significant difference between the story of the Hummingbird and the Crane—set down from Creek, Natchez Cherokee, Alabama, Koasati, and Hichiti[2] sources in SMTS—and the Cherokee telling of it in MMOC (pp. 290-91): in the latter myth the birds are not racing merely to ascertain which one is faster; the prize is a young woman.

A Natchez Cherokee relation that we recorded faithfully follows the standard pattern of the Southeast; but we also captured from Siquanid' an entirely different, apparently never before recorded story that considerably embellishes this Cherokee theme of the amorous rivalry of the dapper and agile Hummingbird and the plain and graceless Crane.

The Hummingbird and the Crane Race

The Hummingbird said to the Crane, "I can outfly you," and the Crane said, "No, you can't outfly me."

So they had a race.

All day long they raced, and that night the Hummingbird[3] slept somewhere, but the Crane just kept going. He traveled all night. And then the next day the Hummingbird passed him. Then when it got dark, the Hummingbird found another place to sleep, but the Crane kept on going all night. The Hummingbird rested again the next night; the Crane kept on going.

The Crane arrived at the water [the goal?] first. At dawn the Hummingbird arrived. The Hummingbird lost the race. The Crane was so much faster because he didn't stop at night to sleep.

Tlutlu

The Crane and the Hummingbird: *Rivals*

We shall talk about the Crane and the Hummingbird:

In olden times the Crane was very clever. He always rolled his pants-legs up to his knees. He was a fisherman: he fished for crayfish and fish.

The Hummingbird was living in those days. He was very youthful, and he always wore a necktie. His necktie was shiny, and he always wore a suit. His clothes were blue-black and shiny.

All the young women loved the Hummingbird. When they saw him, they all began to yell, "The Hummingbird is coming! The Hummingbird is coming!" These young women loved him very much because he was so good-looking.

The parents of these young women told them not to be attracted to the Hummingbird. "You shouldn't do that [permit themselves to be attracted?]. You see, it's only his looks that you see. He doesn't work. He wouldn't hunt any food for you if you married him," the parents advised the young women.

The young women didn't believe that. They disliked the Crane who went by every day carrying his fish, but the Crane always gave the parents some fish.

Some time later the Hummingbird married the prettiest of the young women. After they were married, they remained in their house all the time and frolicked.

The Crane had also asked for the hand of one of the daughters but had been refused. "You are so ugly! You're not a good [eligible, suitable] man," the young woman had told the Crane, and that was at the time that the Hummingbird had asked to marry her.

After the Hummingbird did marry her, they frolicked in their house all the time. The young woman kept admiring his handsomeness.

Then one day the beautiful young woman became hungry, but the Hummingbird had never thought of a way to get any food. She said to him, "You don't think about anything except your looks. I'm going to leave you."

So she left the Hummingbird. She went over to the Crane's house.

When she arrived there, she said to the Crane, "I have decided that you can have me. So let's get married and we can eat together then because you are the only one who knows how to get food. I see you carrying your food by every day."

The Crane said, "But I tried to marry you once, and you rejected me. It would be better for you to go back to the Hummingbird." The Crane was piqued.

That's the reason why the Hummingbird and the Crane are not friends. They say that they do not fly together. It is said that the Hummingbird will peck the neck of the Crane when he finds him about his [the Hummingbird's] nesting-place. They say that the Hummingbird does not like for him to come around, and that they always have a fight.

That's all.

Siquanid'

ANIMAL STORIES

ᏔᎦᎬ ᏆᏲᏗ ᎣᎥᏗᎬ ᎣᏌᏯᎢᏐᏱᏗ
ᎢᏱ ᎭᎠᏃ ᏗᏐ ᏆᏬᏎ

"A long time ago . . . it was amazing . . . the Bear
and the Rabbit . . . "

ANIMAL STORIES

BR'ER RABBIT ET ALII

Enough has already been written on the Rabbit as the para-mount animal trickster-figure of the Indians of the Southwest to permit us to move on to the raising of the intriguing question as to why the American Fox is so obtuse whereas his European rela-tive is the epitome of astuteness. One also wonders why the Terra-pin gets such preferential billing among the Cherokees—although one does not wonder why the Bear is portrayed as a good, solid animal citizen, for that's what he is.

(We have no doubt that the Wolf as the dupe in the first ver-sion of "Fireless Cookers" was a relatively recent substitute for the Fox. In other days the Wolf, totemic to one of the clans, was revered. Practically the same may be said of the Deer.)

One regrets the absence of stories about certain animals—the Squirrel, for instance. But the real regret is not that this or that beast has no representation; it is that such a great part of the teem-ing world of Cherokee mythology, under the very windows of the scholar's study, was allowed to slip away forever.

The Tail and the Wags

Most compilations of Southeastern stories suffer from both un-fortunate omission and distressful addition: the little musical inter-polations have not been preserved, and the characteristically lean Indian speech has been fleshed out in the translation with rotundi-ties as meet as whipped cream on hominy.

Our version of the myth in explanation of the appearance of the tail of the Possum we recorded in the Itsôdiyi community of Adair

15

County. Since it contains a scrap of music, we can but wonder what
was lost by Mooney's failure to set down the more extensive musical
inserts in his relation of this myth in MMOC (p. 269).[1]

And we trust that we have refrained here from the gilding of
the linguistic lily: this is Yan'sa's narrative style, not the authors'.

Why the Possum's Tail Is Bare

I am going to begin with a Possum story:

A long time ago the Possum was beautiful. He himself thought
that he was the most beautiful of all the animals. His tail was
beautiful: it was bushy and flowing. Before he retired every night,
he combed his tail, and this made the hair on it shiny and smooth.
When he arose early in the morning, he combed his tail and danced
and sang about his beautiful tail:

He   nio   dil'   dil'   ha   qua   que   la   lo!

That's what he was saying when he was singing about his tail:

He   nio   dil'   dil'   ha   qua   que   la   lo![2]

All of the animals hated him when they heard him bragging so
much. Sometime later they asked an insect called the Ats' [Moth]
to go to see the Possum and cut all the hair off his tail.

"You must go at night," they told him. There was a small
stream and he couldn't cross it; so he returned without doing anything.

The second time, the Cricket was asked: "You must cut the
hair off his tail."

So he went. He crossed the creek, and when he arrived there
[at the home of the Possum], the Possum was asleep, and the
Possum never knew that the hair of his tail was cut off.

The hair [though actually severed] was still on the tail. Next morning the Possum arose and got his comb. He combed his tail, and the comb scraped away all the hair.

He laughed and said, "He!"

That's why the Possum has a slick tail.

Yan'sa

The Racing Terrapin

Indian mythology is laden with great quantities of impossible races by unlikely opponents under improbable conditions. There are recorded in MMOC, SMTS, and SCIT no less than eleven different tellings of that great favorite of the Southeastern Indians, the story of the race between the Terrapin (or Turtle) and some intrinsically speedier animal—variously the Rabbit, the Deer, or the Wolf.

Now to this body of material we add three new versions of the race and one new animal, the fast but equally futile Fox.

The Rabbit and the Terrapin Race

Long ago the Rabbit and the Terrapin had a race. They had a long way to go, and each hoped he would win.

They crossed valleys and high hills, and at the top of each hill a new terrapin started. That's the way they did throughout the entire race. (There was only one rabbit, but there were many terrapins—a different one who started at each hilltop.) Therefore the Rabbit was left behind.

So the Terrapin won the race.

That's all.

Tsiwôn'

The Terrapin and the Deer Race

The Terrapin and the Deer wanted to have a race. The Terrapin said, "I am going to wear a white corn-shuck on my head."

So he gathered his friends and told them that they were to

station themselves at the top of each hill over which the race was to be run. So at each hilltop sat a terrapin exactly like the others.

When they [the Terrapin and the Deer] started the race, they went downhill, then uphill, and at the top sat the "Terrapin." Then when they went down in the valley again, then up the hill, there sat the terrapin who had arrived there already. Then when they went down and up the third time, there he [the "Terrapin"] sat already.

The Terrapin won the race, they say. He used his friends with corn-shucks just like he had and placed them at intervals.

That's all.

Tlutlu

The Terrapin and the Fox Race

The Terrapin and the Fox had a race. (In those days everything could talk: the birds could talk, the squirrels could talk, everything could talk—*even shoes*[3] could talk.) The Terrapin and the Fox boasted to each other about how well they could run.

"Let's have a race," they said. They wagered a small amount of money.

The Terrapin was very clever. He sought out friends that closely resembled him and placed them at the top of each of *seven ridges*.[4] Whoever reached the top of the *seven ridges* was to whoop, "Hut! Hut!"

"Let's get together. Let's start at the same time," they said.

The Fox spread his tail out flat upon the ground. The Terrapin had his friends posted upon the various ridges. (He was cheating the Fox because the Terrapin was really very slow.) He had told his friends to "Hut! Hut!" at [the top of] each ridge.

So when the Fox got to the [top of the] first ridge, he whooped, but the "Terrapin" on the second ridge gave a whoop.

The original Terrapin had remained at the starting place. When the Fox arrived at the goal of the race, one of the terrapins was already there: the Fox was defeated.

Ever' time this Fox, he whoop, in [on] *next ridge the Terrapin*

was whooping ahead of him. The Fox lost; the Terrapin won the
bet.

Dôi

The Racing Crayfish

We garnered three narrations of as preposterous an athletic contest as one could imagine, a race between the Fox and the Crayfish
(one raconteur substituted the Terrapin for the Crayfish, a move
which makes the story no less ludicrous). The only notation of
this little absurdity in SMTS is from a Natchez Cherokee source,
as is our first version. Swanton ascribes to it a European influence
(see TMIF, p. 235).

In its original language, the third version offered here fairly
dances with merriment in Siquanid' 's telling of it. It bubbles along
over a bed of subtle linguistic pebbles that can but be hinted at
in the translation. In its felicitous phraseology and its dramatic
telling it is a masterpiece of Cherokee folk-humor.

The Crayfish and the Fox Race (I)

When they [the Crayfish and the Fox] had a race, the Crayfish said, "You can't outrun me."

"I can outrun you," said the Fox. "When I say, 'Now!'⁵ we'll
go," said the Fox.

When they started the race, the Crayfish got upon the Fox's
tail and said to the Fox, "When we get there [the goal], we must
make a quick turn."

So when they arrived [at the goal], the Fox made a quick turn,
and when he did that, the Crayfish got off the tail [of the Fox].

The Crayfish won the race, they say. He had gotten on the
tail [of the Fox] and gotten off the tail [of the Fox].

That's all: it [the story] was a short one.

Tlutlu

The Fox and the Terrapin Race

When the Fox and the Terrapin had a race, the Fox spread his tail out flat, the Terrapin quietly got upon it, and the Fox carried him away.

When they arrived at the seventh ridge, the Fox gave a quick turn. The Terrapin got off and said, "I beat you!"

"But you're so strange-looking! You look like somebody else. You have red eyes. You're not the one that I made a bet with!" said the Fox.

"Yes, I am. You see, I ran so fast in the race that the dust and the wind got into my eyes and made them red," he [the Terrapin] said as he lied.

The Fox lost. The Terrapin was riding. (Laugh.) Yes, he was carried.

Dôi

The Crayfish and the Fox Race (II)

Once the Crayfish was out of the water, walking around in the mud near the water. The Fox was sitting very near him. They began to talk, and the Fox asked the Crayfish, "How can you get out of the water and walk so fast upon the ground?"

The Crayfish said, "I'm very fast. If I had to run a race, I could do so right now."

The Fox said, "What can you do to run a race? You're so slow that you'd just crawl."

"Well, if you don't believe me, I'll run you a race," said the Crayfish.

"All right,"⁶ said the Fox. "Let's do [race]."

The Crayfish said, "All right. We'll run across seven ridges, and whoever reaches the seventh one first will whoop."

"All right," said the Fox.

So they got up and went to the top of a high mountain from where they would have to go down and up, down and up seven times.

As they started the race, they were standing even with each other on the starting line. When they started, the Crayfish was rather slow getting off. The Fox was ahead of him, all but for his tail. As they whooped and got started, the Fox's tail flew right by the Crayfish who grasped the very end of the tail and got upon it.

The Fox was racing as hard as he could—he was really the only one in the race because the Crayfish was riding his tail—and when they got to the seventh ridge and the Fox whooped, there beside him whooped the Crayfish.

The Fox said to the Crayfish, "You certainly are fast!"

"I told you so," said the Crayfish. "I'm very fast, and I race frequently."

The Fox said, "We'll race some more—seven more rounds."

So they turned around to run again, and the Crayfish got upon the tail again. When they arrived at the seventh ridge, the Fox whooped, and right beside him whooped the Crayfish.

On their seventh round, about halfway, the Crayfish nearly fell off the tail, and he decided to seat himself upon the tail more firmly. As he was trying to seat himself better, he accidentally grasped the bony part of the tail.

So they arrived at the seventh and last ridge and the Fox whooped, turned around to the Crayfish, and said, "You're cheating me!"

"Certainly not!" said the Crayfish. "That's how fast I am."

The Fox said, "I felt it when you pinched my tail, and I knew you were upon my tail!"

So they went around and around and around, the Fox chasing the Crayfish. But the Crayfish couldn't get away, and the Fox champed him up and ate him.

Siquanid'

A Passion for Peanuts

We have as yet encountered no story, published or unpublished, in the folklore of the Southeastern Indians that appears to be a cognate of this Natchez Cherokee item. It emits an aura that is somehow essentially non-Cherokee. The motif of an animal removing an eye, to point out one dissonance, is atypically Cherokee, albeit it is found among Indians of the Plains, Great Basin, and Pacific Northwest, and also among the Creeks.[7] We venture the guess that the prototype of this story, now possibly lost, was Muskhogean, most likely Creek or Hichiti.

The Rabbit and His "Friend"

The Rabbit wanted some peanuts cooked, but he wasn't allowed to have any.

He said [to his wife, is the implication], "I'm going to the ball game. A 'friend' of mine will arrive here. You must cook him dinner—and you might cook him some peanuts—and when he finishes eating, tell him to come on over [to the ball game]," he said as he left.

When he had walked some distance from the house, he took out one of his eyes. (He had said to his wife, "You will certainly know him [the spurious friend] because he has one eye.") Sure enough, he took out his eye, put it upon a stump, left it there, and went back home. When he got home, he truly was fed all the peanuts he wanted.[8]

(No! When he arrived, he had two eyes because when the "friend" arrived, it was he who arrived. The peanuts had been cooked, and he ate all he wanted and then left. He wanted to tell a lie about it, so he took out his eye.)

"They hit me in the eye at the ball game and made me blind forever."

This was the story that he wanted people to believe, they say. *That's all.*

Tlutlu

Little Thief, Petit Larceny

In SMTS are to be found two Creek myths and one Natchez Cherokee in explanation of the thieving propensities of the Rabbit. Our story, recorded for us by an elderly Natchez Cherokee who is a nephew of the man who was Swanton's informant of half a century ago, strangely enough bears a far closer resemblance to one of the aforementioned Creek versions than it does to that of his uncle.

The Natchez Cherokee myth in SMTS introduces the persons of the Alligator, a beast outside of the purlieus of Cherokee story-material. The other Creek story, highly synoptic, substitutes the Possum for the Rabbit.

Why the Rabbit Steals

When everything was distributed, the Rabbit chose the *sycamore* because it bore so many seeds. He thought he would always have food to eat. All the others [the other animals] took everything else.

So the Rabbit kept waiting for those seeds to fall, but instead of falling, they were blown away by the wind. He didn't have anything to eat.

So he went to the King[9] who had distributed the food supply and told him about the tree and that he [the Rabbit] had nothing to eat.

Then the King said, "If you'll bring me something I like, I'll give you something else."

He [the Rabbit] went out to hunt something, but whatever he brought the King didn't like. He couldn't find anything that the King liked.

So the Rabbit told the King, "I just can't find anything that the King would like to eat."

The King said, "All right."

The Rabbit then said, "I'll just have to go eat up old women's gardens. I'll eat up their cabbage and just steal everything. They'll have their dogs chase me," he said as he chose that [garden vegetables] for his food.

That's why he is a garden-thief.

That's all.

Tlutlu

The Rabbit as Aerialist

The motif of the duck-hunting Rabbit is a minor one, but it runs merrily through Koasati, Natchez Cherokee,[10] and Cherokee (East and West)[11] sources. We taped a telling of the Oklahoma myth in Cherokee County, within a few miles of Tahlequah, where Mooney obtained his some three-quarters of a century ago. It is interesting to note how little sea-change it has suffered within this space of time.

The Rabbit, the Mink, and the Woodpecker[12]

There were ducks in a large river. On the bank, watching them, was the Rabbit. After a while the Mink arrived and said, "Sometimes I just get so very hungry"—the ducks were still in the water, away off—"that I could go catch one of those ducks," he said.

"Let's see you," said the Rabbit.

So the Mink dived into the water, went underwater until he reached the ducks, seized one of them by the leg, and pulled it [the duck] through the water until he reached the bank where the Rabbit was.

"See what I can do?" said the Mink.

The Rabbit said, "Well, I can do that, too."

"Let's see you go get one," said the Mink.

So the Rabbit dived in, but he couldn't go underwater all the way to where the ducks were. He had to poke his nose above water. When he reached the ducks, he seized one by the leg, but he frightened them all, and they all flew away.

The one that he had hold of also flew away and pulled him through the air. The duck carried the Rabbit away off across a mountain. While he was flying over this mountain, the Rabbit lost his grip and fell down into a hollow tree. The Rabbit remained [imprisoned] in there.

After a while he heard the Woodpecker pecking upon the outside of the tree.

"Keep pecking at it and make the hole large because I'm a

beautiful animal and the children like me and like to play with me,"[13] said the Rabbit. So the Woodpecker worked very hard and made a large hole.

After a while the Rabbit said, "Get out of the way! Let me see the hole!"

When the Rabbit looked out of the hole, he leaped out and ran away. When he went through the hole, almost all of his hair was scraped off, but he whooped as he ran off. (Laugh.)

Gahnô

On Lending Without Collateral

One would think that the myth transcribed below might contain all of the elements requisite for its dissemination over the whole Southeastern area; but it is to be found only in MMOC and MMOC (1888), to our knowledge, although Gilbert states in GTEC that he collected it in Big Cove on the Eastern Cherokee Reservation. Our Natchez Cherokee recitation of it varies appreciably from that of Mooney.

This is one of the few myths in which the Rabbit himself is duped.

The Deer Steals From the Rabbit

In this one [story] the Deer said to the Rabbit, "You certainly do have beautiful shoes (the Deer wanted them). Why don't you lend them to me for a while, and I'll run about in them."

The Rabbit said, "You might run off with them."

The Deer said, "No."

So the Rabbit lent him the shoes, and the Deer ran about and then came back. "These are just perfect for running in the woods," he said as he came back. And then he said, "Let me run farther."

But the Rabbit liked his shoes, so he said, "You might run away with them."

"No," he [the Deer] said. "I want everything—your hat and your shoes (the horns that the Rabbit had on was his hat)."

So the Rabbit lent these things to him [the Deer], and the Deer ran off with them forever. They say that at one time the Rabbit's feet were the Deer's.[14]

That's all.

Tlutlu

One Man's Meat, Another Man's Poison

The theme of the ensuing story is one of the major ones of American Indian folklore. Boas[15] discovered it among no less than forty-one different tribes, to which number Swanton[16] contributed seven additional ones. We add to this pool four Cherokee variants, the first of which was recorded about three miles north of Barber in Cherokee County, the next two in Nuwôtûn' Ukedaliyû in western Adair County, and the fourth a couple of miles or so northwest of Bunch in Adair County.

In the matter of detail, they complement each other.

The Rabbit Imitates the Bear

The Bear met the Rabbit. The Rabbit asked the Bear why he [the Bear] was so fat: "Where do you get your grease?"

"Just most anywhere. I can cut myself in the chest and get some," the Rabbit was told.

When the Rabbit tried [to duplicate the Bear's feat], he accidentally cut his nose.[17] He fell down, rolled over a time or two, and fainted. He didn't find any grease [in himself].

That's all.

Dalala (N.)

The Buzzard[18] Doctors the Rabbit (I)

Long ago, the Rabbit became ill.[19] All of his friends were watching over him. They decided to find a doctor for him. They found the Buzzard.

The Buzzard said, "I'll doctor him, but he must be alone. There is to be no one going in or out."

So the door was closed, and the Rabbit's friends were on the outside. They heard the Rabbit cry, "Duwi!" and later on the Buzzard opened the door, dashed out, and flew up into the sky. He flew so high that he got away from the Rabbit's friends.

"He has killed him! There is nothing but bones left!" they cried.

The friends said that the Buzzard had done wrong because he was supposed to have been a doctor. But they couldn't get [punish] him because he flew too far away.

Now the Terrapin decided that he would kill the Buzzard, so he turned over on his back and used his feet to shoot his arrow in the direction in which the Buzzard had gone.[20]

Now the friends never knew whether or not the arrow ever hit the Buzzard, but they did know that their friend the Rabbit was dead and that the Terrapin had tried to help [?] the Rabbit by attempting to kill the Buzzard.

That's all I know.[21]

Ganahw'sôsg'

The Rabbit, the Bear, and the Buzzard

The Rabbit and the Bear lived many years ago. The Bear was fat, and the Rabbit was lean.

One day they cooked beans. They decided that they needed some seasoning for the beans. Since the Bear was fat, he cut himself in the side and used his fat as a seasoning for the beans.

Later on, when the Bear was visiting the Rabbit, the Rabbit decided that he would try to get some fat off himself for his seasoning, but he nearly killed himself because he was so lean.

The Rabbit decided that he needed a doctor, so the Bear went for one. He met the Crow first.

"I'm not a doctor," said the Crow, "because I have black legs."[22]

Then later the Bear met the Terrapin. The Bear asked him if he could doctor.

The Terrapin said, "No. I have red eyes."

Still later he met the Buzzard.

"Yes, I'm a doctor," said the Buzzard.

Then the Bear said, "All right. Come with me."

So they went to the Rabbit's house, and the Buzzard said, "When I doctor, all the doors must be closed."

When the Buzzard closed the door, he began eating the Rabbit. While he was being eaten, the Rabbit cried, "Ayô!"[23] because of the pain.

The Bear said, "Now why is the Rabbit making those noises?"

"He is making those noises because every time I rub him it hurts him," said the Buzzard.

That's all.

Tsiwôn'

The Buzzard Doctors the Rabbit (II)

A long time ago . . . it was amazing . . . the Bear and the Rabbit . . .

The Rabbit went to the Bear's house on Sunday, and when he wanted to leave, he was asked to stay for dinner because the Bear was cooking beans. The Rabbit decided to stay.

The Bear was cooking beans, and when the beans were done, the Bear stabbed himself in the side and poured the grease from it [his side] into the beans. They ate well.

When it was time for the Rabbit to leave, he said, "You must come to see me Sunday."

The Bear said, "All right."

So next Sunday the Bear went to the home of the Rabbit. The Rabbit was cooking beans. He knew how the Bear had gotten his grease, so he stabbed his [the Rabbit's] side to try to get some grease. But wasn't successful. Instead he fell over.

"What did you do to yourself?" said the Bear to the Rabbit. "You see, I'm very fat. That's the reason I can do that [obtain grease in that fashion]. I'll go find you a doctor."

On the way he saw the Crow upon a limb. He said to him, "Would you have any medicine for those who have stabbed themselves in the side?"

"I don't know anything. I have yellow legs,"[24] said the Crow.

He went on. Then he saw the Buzzard sitting upon a limb. He asked him, "Would you know any medicine for those who have stabbed themselves in the side?"

The Buzzard said, "I'm an expert in treating those whose sides are stabbed." So the Bear took the Buzzard to where the Rabbit was.

"Close all the doors—that's the way I do when I doctor."

So all the animals went outside except the Bear[25] and the Rabbit. The Buzzard began to eat the Rabbit. Every once in a while he [the Rabbit] would say, "Ayô!" and the animals who were waiting outside would ask the Buzzard, "What's wrong with the Rabbit?" and he [the Buzzard] would say, "It hurts him when I thump him [in examining his injury]."

"All right. I'm through," said the Buzzard as he came out and flew away up in the air.

The animals came in and found the Rabbit all eaten up. Only bones were left.

The animals missed him [the Buzzard] with their bows and arrows as he flew up in the air. The Terrapin was there, and he said, "Let me have a bow and arrow."

"You can't do anything. He's too high," they told him.

Finally they decided to give him a bow and arrow. He turned over [upon his back] and shot him [the Buzzard] right in the nose. When he [the Terrapin] shot him [the Buzzard] in the nose, this caused the Buzzard to fall down right at their [the animals'] feet.

That's the way it was. That's why it was amazing a long time ago.

Sgequa

(*Verbal Note on the Tape*)

ANNA G. KILPATRICK: That's the reason why his [the Buzzard's] nostrils are so large?

SGEQUA: Yes. That's why he has such large nostrils.

Fireless Cookers

This story would not seem to appear anywhere in the literature of the Southeast, although the motif of the detached tail thrust into the ground does. In the Dalala (N.) version the Rabbit is replaced by Maneater and the Wolf by the Fox. In Muskhogean stories Maneater is usually equated with some large member of the cat family, but the teller of this tale makes a point of Maneater's human attributes, and one infers a being somewhat like Tseg'sgin' (see the chapter "Tseg'sgin' Stories").

The Rabbit Dupes the Wolf

Now somewhere the Rabbit and the Wolf had killed a cow. They prepared it for cooking, then they fried it.

(No, they didn't! They wanted to broil it but found that they didn't have any fire.)

By the time they had it all cut up, it was very late, and the sun was nearly down. When it is very late, it gets red in the west.

Now the Rabbit had an idea for putting the Wolf to work. He said to the Wolf, "Go find that fire that we can see in the west where that red area is."

The Wolf agreed to go, and went. He went down the hill, then he went up the hill, and when he got to the top, he could see that he had the same distance to go to find that red area that he thought was fire.

He continued on. He went uphill, then downhill. He still had the same distance to go. He continued going uphill and downhill, and the distance [to the red area] was so far!

Finally he became tired, because when he went up the hill, the distance to the red area was the same.

He finally gave up and returned to where the Rabbit was. The Rabbit had already moved the meat, and the Wolf couldn't find it. The Rabbit had played a trick on him. The Rabbit just wanted to hide the meat.

This is what the Rabbit told the Wolf: "I went away awhile, and when I returned, the meat was all gone. Somebody got it."

The Wolf was thoroughly duped, and there was nothing he could do about it. The Rabbit was very tricky!

That's the end of what I know about that.

Yan'sa

Maneater Dupes the Fox

Maneater was leading a cow. The cow that he was leading was very fat.

The Fox came up and said, "Let's kill her, and we'll eat."

"But there's no fire; we can't cook her," he [Maneater] told the Fox.

When the sun is very low in the west, it makes a very red area. That's the way it was at the time they were talking.

Maneater said to the Fox, "If you'll go get that fire that we see in the west, we'll cook."

So the Fox left to hunt the fire. He went a long way, but he couldn't find the fire, so he returned.

When the Fox returned, he found Maneater on his knees down on the ground, pulling at the cow's tail which was stuck in the ground. When the Fox returned, he said, "I couldn't find the fire. I crossed a hundred valleys, but each time I came on top of a hill, it was the same distance [to the fire]," said the Fox.

"That's just our luck," Maneater said, "because our cow went under the ground!" He was pulling on the tail. He said to the Fox, "You help me pull. Maybe we can pull her out."

So the Fox helped Maneater, and they pulled and pulled. Maneater somehow had the tail fastened to the ground. It loosened, pulled out, and they fell backward.

Maneater said, "Well, there is nothing we can do now. She has disappeared into the ground."

While the Fox had gone to hunt the fire, Tseg'nudan'tun'[26] had quickly killed the cow and put the meat away in a tree.

As he looked at the tail on the ground, the Fox was pondering about this [ruse?]. The meat that had been hung high up in the tree fell down. It hit the Fox on the back and killed him.

That's all. (Laugh.)

Dalala (N.)

(Verbal Note on the Tape)

ANNA G. KILPATRICK: What did you say—the Fox and what?

DALALA: Maneater.

A.G.K.: What did he look like?

D.: He was like a person, a person who can talk. He lived long ago.

Turkey Dinner, Thanks to the Rabbit

The following story is rather remarkable for being so widespread and for having enjoyed so many mutations in the course of its travels. Tellers of the tale among the various tribes of the Southeast agree but poorly as to what animals were involved in it, but the plot remains constant.[27]

In two of our variants the Wildcat, cast most often as the dupe, is significantly replaced. Despite the fact that this beast gets star billing in the MMOC version, one gets the impression that in Cherokee mythology, viewed broadly, the Wildcat is fortunate to get a walk-on part.

Our second version, Natchez Cherokee, loudly proclaims its Muskhogean lineage. Muskhogean animals, to cite but one revealing detail, are given to expressing disgust by plucking out and throwing away one of their eyes.[28] This motif is unknown, or as yet unknown, in Cherokee oral tradition.

The Rabbit Dupes the Fox

Long ago, when the old people were talking, I listened.

The Rabbit met the Fox. The Rabbit was afraid [of the Fox], so he said, "Don't kill me because, you see, I saw some turkeys wandering around as I came by."

[The answer of the Fox is missing here.]

The Rabbit said, "All right, then; you must pretend to be dead, then I'll put some drops of spunk-water in your eyes."

So the Fox agreed to lie down and permit drops to be put into his eyes, and then when the Fox lay down upon the ground, the Rabbit put drops into the Fox's eyes. The Rabbit told the Fox to sing to himself while he was lying down, pretending to be dead: "I'm going to get the gobbler as he walks by."

Well, when the turkeys came by and the Fox was singing his song, the Rabbit seized the gobbler and ran off.

That's all I know.

Ganahw'sôsg'

The Rabbit Dupes the Wildcat

The Rabbit noticed that the Wildcat was getting ready to pounce upon him, so the Rabbit said, "The things you always eat are down the road. You must lie down here and pretend to be dead, and I'll go get them."

He did go get the gobblers, several of them. The Wildcat was upon the ground pretending to be dead.

"You must dance around him and torment him, and I will sing for you," said the Rabbit. So the gobblers began to dance around the Wildcat. Said the Rabbit as he sang:

Di- ga- tsa- li! Tsa- la- ka- li- sa! Sa- ma- lo- ha!²⁹

"Is that how you sing it [the song]?" asked the gobblers.

"That's it. That's how I sing all night long," he said.

So when the gobblers drew very near to the Wildcat, he seized one by the legs. When he seized him [the gobbler] by the legs, the turkey flew and pulled the Wildcat with him. He dropped the Wildcat into a valley.

The Wildcat's eye had accidentally been pulled out [of the socket]. Looking up, he was attempting to replace it [in the socket]. There was someone standing above him nearby.

"Did he injure you very much?" he [the "someone"] asked.

When the Wildcat heard this, he pulled his eye all the way out, threw it away, and ran on down the valley, they say.

That's all.

Tlutlu

The Rabbit and the Possum Dine on Turkey

Now the Rabbit got hungry. He wanted turkey. He encountered the Possum.

When the Possum and the Rabbit talked: "Now you must lie down here and pretend that you are dead," said the Rabbit. "I'll go get the turkeys. You can have first choice if you will lie down and pretend to be dead."

"All right," said the Possum as he lay down. The turkeys . . . no, I mean the Rabbit went to where the turkeys were.

"Yonder down the road is a Possum lying dead. So you come with me, and you must dance around him. You must torment him."

Single file, the turkeys approached the Possum.

"Now dance, then go all around him; and sometimes you must kick him as I sing," said the Rabbit as he seated himself a short distance away.

So the turkeys began to go around and around the Possum, and sometimes they kicked him.

The Rabbit was singing as he sat nearby:

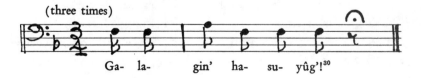

(three times)

Ga- la- gin' ha- su- yûg'![30]

That's what he was saying as he sang.

Sure enough, in a little while the Possum reached out his arm, took a gobbler by the leg, and killed him.

The Rabbit just wanted something for both of them to eat because he was hungry and wanted turkey. So they dined—the Possum and the Rabbit.

The Rabbit is very tricky—even today he is very tricky.

That's all.

Yan'sa

The Cherokee Uncle Remus

One of the finest animal stories in the whole range of Cherokee folklore is the best known of all—that of the Rabbit and the sticky statue. Borrowed from the Indians by Negro slaves, it was obtained from the Negroes and put into the literary consciousness of the whole world by Joel Chandler Harris (1848-1908) in his "Uncle Remus" tales. Although it was widely known over aboriginal America, it was (and still is) a prime favorite of the Cherokees.

Our second version of it is one of the choicest items obtained in our field-work. In the original language it is a superb job of storytelling, and we deeply deplore the inevitable loss of so much in the process of translation. The felicitous choice of words, the depth of role characterization through vocal inflection, and the power of conveyance through body-movement can be but hinted at in prosaic literal transliteration. We hope that a sufficient residue remains to give some illusion of being in the presence of as consummate a master of his art as still lives among his people.

The Rabbit and the Image

The Maneaters[31] were going to dig a well. There had been no rain, and it was very dry.

The Rabbit came up and asked, "What are all of you doing?"

"We are digging a well for water. Help us, and we can all use it," he was told.

"No. I can find water whenever I need it. You see, I can find mine in the dew."

When he refused [their request], they told him, "All right, when we find our water, don't you be stealing it."

The Rabbit said, "All right, I'll find mine in the dew."

Then the Rabbit left, but that very night he came and got [some of] their water. They found out that they had lost some water, and they said, "We'll assume that the Rabbit did it." And then the following night they lost some more water.

Well, they set a trap for him [the Rabbit]. They set up something in the shape of a person, very sticky. Even if you accidentally touched it, you would be stuck fast to it.

When on the third night the Rabbit came to get some more water, he saw the image standing there. The Rabbit said to it, "Who are you? Move out of the way!"

He kept saying this to the image. The image remained silent.

"Aren't you going to answer me?" he [the Rabbit] said, and hit it [the image] with his fist. The Rabbit became stuck to the image.

Well, he tried to get loose, but he couldn't, and he kept saying, "Let me go! Let me go!" Then he hit the image with his other fist, and that became stuck. Now both arms were stuck.

Well, the next morning when the Maneaters came, they found the Rabbit hanging to the image. They took him off [the image] and said, "We're going to kill him, aren't we?"

"Yes, I'd be glad if you'd kill me," said the Rabbit.

The Maneaters decided not to kill him since he said that he would like to be killed. Then the Maneaters said, "Let's throw him in that huge pile of brush."

The Rabbit said, "I'd like that even better."

"Well, then," they said, "let's just whip him with switches."

Then the Rabbit said, "I'd like that even better."

Then the Maneaters said, "Let's throw him in that dense briar patch."

The Rabbit howled and cried.

So they swung him by his arms over to the briar patch. When they threw him into the briar patch, he whooped and ran away from them. (Laugh.)

That's all I know of that.

Dalala (N.)

The Rabbit and the Bear

We'll tell one more—the Rabbit and the Bear:

A long time ago, when animals could talk, the Rabbit was exceedingly finicky. He was like a young man who is a dandy— always clean, wearing gloves and white clothes. The Rabbit was just like a young man—elegant!

The Bear was a hard worker.

There was a drought at that time, so the Bear gathered all of them [the animals] together: all of the flying creatures; even the cows; and the Wolf, the Fox, and the Buzzard. He gathered all of the flying creatures[32] together, and the Bear preached to them:

"We're going to search for water, since we don't have any," he said, "—if you think it is all right to do so. When we search for this water, we'll have a gadug'[33] and we'll dig a deep well," said the Bear.

All of these wild animals thought it was good to do this because they didn't have any water. So they all had to help, and the Rabbit with his elegant clothes on was just going by, back and forth.

Finally they stopped the Rabbit. "What are you going by here for? We're having a meeting. We're going to search for water, and it would benefit you, too. We'll all drink it," they said. That's what the Rabbit was told when he was stopped.

"My clothes would get dirty, and I don't like for my hands to get dirty," said the Rabbit as he went on.

"When we find some water, you can't have any to drink," the Rabbit was told.

"That's all right. I get my water early in the morning from the dew. I put my pails under the leaves," said the Rabbit.

So they called this gadug'[34] and began to dig the well. The Bear
was the foreman. There were many of them [the animals] digging
away down deep in the ground, and they had a ladder down there
to them, and these diggers down there could see that there was a
little water coming up. (It was very far down there.) After they
got more water to come in and they got out, they left the ladder
to use when they went to get the water.

The Rabbit began to think about how he could steal their water
(but if anyone stole the water, he was to be killed if he had not
taken part in digging for it). He went [to the well] very early,
before dawn. He took small bottles with him. He went down the
ladder and got the water.

When he reached home, he put his water in pottery vessels that
had cuplike handles and set these on shelves, then he thought about
what he would tell someone if he [someone] found out where he
got his water.

So the Bear came one day. The Bear noticed the vessels of water
on the shelves. "Where do you get so much water that you have
stored on the shelves?" asked the Bear.

The Rabbit said, "I put my vessels out at night where the
weeds are high and where there is dew. The next day, when the
sun comes up, my vessels are full of water, and I take them home,"
said the Rabbit.

The Bear didn't quite believe that; so the Bear said, "Let's go
down to the well and see about our water."

So they [the animals] went down the ladder, and when they
reached a ledge where one could walk, there they saw the Rabbit's
footprints.

"There are his tracks! He does steal our water! Let's do something with him; let's set a trap for him."

So they put a trap just at the end of the ladder where he would
step to get the water.

Far into the night the Rabbit came. He went down into the
well. When he looked down to see the water, there he saw the trap,

and he carefully pushed it aside, got the water, and took it home.

The next day the Bear came again. There the Rabbit was sitting, and the Bear looked around and thought, "He got our water again! He's really clever."

So the Bear went back to his friends that had helped him dig the well. He said to them, "I would like you all to think about how we can make the Rabbit stop stealing our water. Let's put a sticky black image of a man down there. If he [the Rabbit] hits it, he'll stick to it, and then if he sticks to it, he'll remain stuck."

"All right," they said.

So they put a black image about as tall as the Rabbit down in the well.

About midnight the Rabbit went to get some more water. He went down the ladder into the well, and when he was halfway down the ladder, he noticed a black shadow standing there.

He stopped, and he thought, "There is someone standing there." So he said, "Heh! Who are you?" he said to the image.

The image was silent.

The Rabbit said, "I'm speaking to you!"

The image stood silent.

"When I speak again and you don't answer, I'm going to hit you!"

More silence.

The third time he questioned, whereupon he immediately struck the black image. His hand stuck, and he couldn't pull it away.

"I'll hit you with my other hand!" said the Rabbit, and he used his other hand and hit it [the image]. Now both hands were stuck.

"I'm going to butt you with my head!" he said. Now his head was stuck. He was stuck in the shape of a ball.

"I can still kick you!" he said. Then he kicked it [the image]. So he was completely stuck.

Early the next morning when they all [the animals] came,

there was the Rabbit down in the well, stuck like a ball. So they got hold of him, tied his legs, and took him home.

When they got him home, they said, "What are we going to do with him? Let's cut off his legs and head," they said, "then we'll throw him away."

The Rabbit thought that was funny. He laughed. "I take my legs off at night when I go to bed, and I take my head off and put it upon the shelf."

"What shall we do with him?" they said.

The Rabbit was thinking. He thought, "When they say, 'Let's throw him into the briar patch!' I'm going to cry very loud."

So the Bear said, "This is what we'll do: We'll tie his legs and head together, find the thickest, prickliest briar patch, and throw him into it."

So immediately the Rabbit cried as nobody had ever cried before.

They [the animals] said, "Let's do that to him!" So they tied his legs[35] and carried him away.

(The Rabbit knew that he could run away after he got into the briar patch.)

So they swung him into the briar patch.

When he landed in the briar patch, he gave a big whoop—he whooped just as hard as he could[36]—and when he hit the ground, he made such a large, deep hole that water spurted up immediately, and when he ran away, he made a crooked path, and the water followed him.

They say that the reason why rivers run in a crooked course today is because that is where the Rabbit ran.[37] He found this water, and they [the animals] had plenty of water then, and the Rabbit was responsible for it.

That's all.

Siquanid'

UK'TEN' STORIES

ᎠᏈᏔᎢᎬᏆᏏᏲᎩᏰᏃ Ꮮ ᎤᏁᏥᎧᏔ ᎥᏯ
ᎢᎤᏯᏘ ᎤᏔᎤᎪ

"Thunder is not fierce, but he is very friendly . . . "

UK'TEN' STORIES

AN UNNECESSARY EVIL

The attributes imputed to the Uk'ten' are strikingly similar to those ascribed to the European dragon. Both are gigantic reptiles with a lethal breath; both frequent marshy or rocky places; both of these horned creatures with claws prey on man. By way of explanation there leaps to mind the outside possibility of a Mesozoic survival up into contemporaneity with the human race.

The Uk'ten' represents to the Cherokees something more than an inimical aspect of nature: to some extent it symbolizes satanic deceit, confusion, and negation. Still, oddly enough, in defeat the power of the Uk'ten' is reversed: the scales of the Uk'ten' provide protection and healing.

Cherokees both East and West can point out the scratches made by Uk'ten's on the surface of rocks. We have never had occasion to see them, and doubt if they would be worth the trouble taken to view them. Far more intriguing to us is the track that the Uk'ten' has etched across the mind of man.

The Serpent of the Cherokee Eden

While the general characteristics of the Uk'ten' seem to be well established, one discovers that there remains room for personal opinions. We have the depositions of a trio of witnesses whose testimony is perforce hearsay, but nonetheless sincere.

Asudi on the Uk'ten'

ANNA G. KILPATRICK: Did you ever hear of the Uk'ten'?

ASUDI: Yes, I have.

A.G.K.: I wonder what it was . . .

A.: It was a snake, a very large snake.

A.G.K.: Where did he live?

A.: I don't know where he lived. He lived somewhere.

A.G.K.: In the water?

A.: Yes, near the larger rivers. When they [human beings] decided to kill him, they used bows and arrows to kill him.

A.G.K.: How did they do it?

A.: He [the one who killed the Uk'ten'] was told to hit him upon the seventh spot. The first time he drew his bow, he missed; the second time he drew his bow, it [the arrow] went under him [the Uk'ten']; on the fourth time that he drew his bow the arrow hit right upon the seventh spot. Then he [the Uk'ten'] fell over and floundered about and tremendous thunder and lightning appeared all about, they say. It continued to thunder and flash lightning.

The Uk'ten' and Thunder were having a fight at that time.[1] That was when Thunder was given help. They [human beings] loved Thunder very much.

The Uk'ten' was very poisonous. One could be killed by walking in his path. These two were fighting to decide which one would live among people. They used bow and arrows to hit him upon the seventh spot. After he fell and floundered about, he caused it to rain hot fire. The fire rained until he was completely dead. The people came from their hiding places after that. They say that's what happened long ago.

This Uk'ten' who lived long ago could have devoured all the people. But that's the way God willed it: that people should live, multiply, and love each other. The reason that we are here is that God is powerful. No man on earth has made things the way they are. It is God, who is so powerful, that has made everything the way it is.

SIQUANID': Yes! Yes!

A.: God decides whether we are to live or not.

Dôi on the Uk'ten'

DOI: Yes, those people who lived long ago were conjurers. They could make themselves appear as something other than what they were, and people fled from them because they were afraid of them. They changed themselves into other things. They could say, "Just let me be this" and they could turn into whatever they wished to be. People were afraid of them. They always ran away.

ANNA G. KILPATRICK: Then the Uk'ten' was not real, he was someone who changed himself into one?

D.: Yes. He just sang his [magic] song and willed himself to be an Uk'ten'.

A.G.K.: Do you mean that he was not really an Uk'ten', that he was just a man?

D.: Yes, that's it! Yes, that's it! He said, "Let me be an Uk'-ten'," and he became one.

A.G.K.: Who were they [these conjurers]?

D.: Just Cherokees.

A.G.K.: What did he [the Uk'ten'] look like?

D.: He was like a snake, I think.

A.G.K.: Did he have horns?

D.: I don't know.

A.G.K.: Is it true that if you merely smelled him, he would kill you?

D.: Yes, that's right. And if an Uk'ten' merely smelled YOU, you'd likewise die. You would ageiyû iwûganug"[2] because he was so fierce.

A.G.K.: Were *Thunder* and the Uk'ten' really fighting?

D.: I never did hear that.

A.G.K.: Do you know of anything [in particular] that the Uk'ten' did?

D.: No.

Yan'sa on the Uk'ten'

YAN'SA: It is very interesting, when one thinks about it, how the Uk'ten' came into being, and when one learns how he met his end.

The Cherokees had from the beginning a reason for killing the

Uk'ten.' When they killed him, when someone shot him, they were after his scales. They [the scales] were to help them [the Cherokees] preserve their race and to ward off evil events; and they [the scales] were what helped them [the Cherokees] in battle.

The Uk'ten' 's scales were not used by the Cherokees only; but several tribes of Indians used them. In war they [the scales] were what they [the Indians] used to help them.

We don't know but that even today somebody may still have the scales of the Uk'ten'. They were kept very much like the uwôd' from the jaw of the lizard.[3] They may have that, too, because there are many, many tribes of brown people.[4]

Defense by Fire

The motif of the seven protective, purifying fires is utterly Cherokeean, and we meet it again in the myth concerning the Uk'ten' and Thunder. The first of the two treatments of the theme appearing here is surely nothing more than a synopsis of the aforementioned myth, the second an excision of an episode from it, supplied with a prelude that is itself doubtless lifted from its context in another and different story.

The Slaying of an Uk'ten'

Now this story is about people of long ago. It must have been [i.e., taken place] before the other story[5] because the Uk'ten' had a spot to lie down in a very dry place.

Now the Cherokees took seven days to select the right way to attack the Uk'ten'. On the seventh day they chose one man to carry the gun.

When morning came, he left to go find where the Uk'ten' was lying. He aimed at the seventh spot. He shot the Uk'ten' once and then returned home. On the next morning he did the same thing.

Now his friends went out and built seven brush arbors spaced out down the road where the youth would run.

On the morning of the seventh day (every morning he shot

the Uk'ten' in the seventh spot) the youth went to shoot the Uk'ten' in the same spot. When he went on the seventh morning, he shot the Uk'ten' in the seventh spot.

As soon as he shot, he ran to the first arbor. The firemakers were running in front of him. The first arbor was already afire, and it was to it that he went.

The fumes from the Uk'ten' arrived at the first arbor just like rain. There was a thundering and roaring.

When that stopped, the youth went on to the second arbor (he ran to the second arbor). In just a short while after he had arrived there, the fumes arrived also, coming again like rain. And the same thing happened at the third [arbor].

When he arrived at the fourth one, it was already burning because the firemakers had set it afire. But the fumes at the fourth one were very faint, like a sprinkle of rain.

So he left there and went on to his friends who were waiting for him and told them all that had happened. Then they all went to see where the Uk'ten' was lying.

When they arrived there, he was apparently dead, and one of the youths who was not very thoughtful grasped the tail of the Uk'ten'.

"This is the way to do him!" he said as he took hold.

The youth's arms fell off; then the flesh fell off all his bones. That's how poisonous an Uk'ten' is!

The Uk'ten' was dead, so they took off all his scales and kept them for the supernatural power that they bestow.

That's all I know of this, but there are other things that I know. I know very little because I have lost so much that I knew.

That's just the way it is.

Yan'sa

The Hunter and the Uk'ten'
I'm going to tell you this one:

A deer hunter went hunting and lost his way. Finally he reached a log cabin where a very old couple lived. This old couple wouldn't allow the deer hunter to go anywhere. When he went hunting, he was permitted to go only for a short while and a short distance.

He would go and return; he did this many times; but one day he went farther [than usual] into the forest. He came to the home of a very old man. He [the deer hunter] wanted to escape; he was a prisoner of these old people.

This old man showed the hunter how to escape. First he gave him [the hunter] an egg, which he took with him. If he were to break this egg somewhere, this would create a river that the old couple could not cross.

So when he broke the egg, he created a river, which he crossed. He also had with him a stone[6] to use just in case they [the old couple] should somehow cross that river. If they did get across the river, he was to throw this stone which would create a huge, high mountain which the old couple could not climb.

After he had done this [broken the egg and thrown the stone], he saw that there was another large river in front of him. He found an Uk'ten' there, and the Uk'ten' said to him, "Get upon my back, and I'll take you across." So he got upon the Uk'ten' 's back, and the Uk'ten' ferried him across.[7] He crossed this very wide river.

After they crossed, the hunter got off the Uk'ten'. They separated there: the man went one way, the Uk'ten' another.

The Uk'ten' was very fierce, given to killing things. He would also kill people, and the people became afraid of him; so they asked the man to kill the Uk'ten'.

The Uk'ten' had seven spots upon his side. The man was told to shoot the Uk'ten' 's seventh spot. He had to make provision ahead of time so that he would be sure to escape from the Uk'ten' and not be harmed.

He made seven fires in the direction in which he would be running. The Uk'ten' was fierce when he emitted his fumes.

So after he did that [made the fires], he took his gun and shot him [the Uk'ten'] in the seventh spot. When he ran to the first fire, it was immediately put out. The fumes of the Uk'ten' did it.

The second fire was put out; the third was not completely extinguished. This went on and on. When he reached the last fire, the seventh one, nothing had happened to the fire, and the man escaped.

Dalala (M.)

The Mighty Rabbit

The story of the Rabbit who cunningly induces a pair of Tie-Snakes[8] to stage a tug of war while each is under the impression that he is pulling against the Rabbit is well represented in the Creek and Hichiti sources of SMTS and the Taskigi of SCIT. Our Natchez Cherokee informant rearranged the details of his story, but its lineage is obvious.

The Rabbit and the Uk'ten'

Long ago there was a Rabbit who was strong and fastidious. He and an Uk'ten' boasted to each other how strong they were (there were large rivers there where the Uk'ten's lived). They set a time to have a tug of war.

"You can't pull me!" said the Rabbit.

"I can pull you!" said the Uk'ten'.

Then they set a definite time to have the tug of war.

So they stretched a grapevine from one river to another. (They set a time [for the contest].)

They were tugging, but they couldn't pull each other out of the water. The grapevine broke.

"See, I told you that you couldn't pull me out of the water!" boasted the Rabbit.

They tied; neither one won the contest.

Tlutlu

The Big One That Got Away

Yan'sa's story of angling for an Uk'ten' has a few rather modern touches, what with its chain and its oxen—conveniences obtained from the Europeans. Since we are dealing here with a people who see no particular inconsistency in eating ganûts' out of Wedgewood or murmuring a spell to ensure the success of a real estate deal, we offer no comment.

The Uk'ten' Caught with a Chain

I am going to tell about the Uk'ten'. This is what I told you about—the Uk'ten'. This is the way I heard it: it was a snake—huge, mighty (now I heard somebody tell about this):

In the ocean, very deep, they saw him lying there. He looked very small, like a lizard would look down in the water, and he had horns like a deer would have. That's the way they saw him.

So they made a strong, long chain. They threw it down in the water, and it caught his horns. Then they got several teams of oxen, and the oxen pulled until his head was above the water. He struggled and pulled all the oxen back. They all fell into the water.

He had deerlike horns. He was a spotted snake with rattles like a rattlesnake. He was spotted like a snake, but he was very huge. I suppose that there is one today who looks like that.

That's all I know about this Uk'ten': he was like a snake, but he had horns like a deer; and upon the horns was where they caught him; and they had a chain, and they had oxen to pull him. (Yes, he pulled the oxen into the water.) He was very much like a snake—just like a rattlesnake, spotted.⁹

From what I have heard, I think that's the way he looked. That's all I know.

Yan'sa

The Friendship of Thunder

The noblest, most moving myth that we heard in our collecting travels was the beautiful relic of the lost national cosmology that deals with the eternal question of the choice between good and evil. It is fitting that the hero-symbol is not that of a man, but that of a child. The choice was made in the innocence of youth, not through knowledge but through pity; and the reward was not power, but love.

Our first version was fragmentary. But Yan'sa's telling of the myth, his magistral Cherokee infused with a biblical simplicity and elevation, fell upon the ears with the runic dignity of a bard's recitation of Beowulf; and clothed in the subtleties of an incomparable skill, Siquanid' 's recounting evoked the breathless atmosphere of the medieval geste told in the shadowy nook of the castle fireplace.

The concept of the guardianship of Thunder over the people with whom he plighted faith in that dim time at the beginning of things is an emotional reality to the Cherokees. They speak of their cosmic friend, Thunder, with the deepest tenderness and reverence.

A corrupt variant of this myth is in MMOC (pp. 300-301) and a sketchy Creek loan-version is on record in SMTS (pp. 7-9), but the complete text of this majestic and touching story, one of the greatest of all American Indian myths, has never before been committed to paper.

Thunder and the Uk'ten' (I)

Long, long ago when they were telling stories, they said that the Uk'ten' was living.

The Uk'ten' and Thunder had a fight. So the Uk'ten' built fires, and Thunder was thundering and making rain, trying to put them out. The Uk'ten' thought that he was going to win this fight, but Thunder overcame him.

Thunder used Lightning to win his fight, they said when they were telling stories long ago.

Tsiwôn'

Thunder and the Uk'ten' (II)

I don't know very much: now I'm very old. I have forgotten a lot, although I've heard a lot of talking that was done long ago about the beginning of things.

For instance, everything used to talk long ago. And also when they were bringing up their boys long ago there were supernaturally wise men, and they also used bows and arrows all the time.

Here is one thing that I have heard about that I have stored away: Thunder and water work together when it rains; and since Thunder is always with us, he and we work together.

Long ago there was a boy out walking, hunting with his bow and arrows. He was on the top of a rough, rugged hill. From where he was, he heard, somewhere down below where it was even more rugged, a thundering, and he was very anxious to find out what caused it.

In looking for it, he arrived down in the valley, and in the ruggedest place [there] Thunder and an Uk'ten' (he was from the sea) had hold of each other in a fierce fight. Thunder was underneath: the Uk'ten' was so long and so strong—that's why he was able to overcome Thunder.

The boy looked at them fighting. (It was thundering very low.) When the boy was seen, when Thunder looked at him, Thunder said, "Nephew, help me! When he looks at you, he will kill you!"

And then the Uk'ten' said, "Nephew, help me! When he thunders, he will kill you!"

They both kept saying these things.

Because Thunder was being bested, the boy felt sorry for him. He decided to shoot at the Uk'ten'. When he shot the Uk'ten', he [the Uk'ten'] was weakened. Then a second time he pulled his bow. The Uk'ten' was weakened even more and Thunder was becoming stronger. He made his thunders louder, and on the fourth thunder, the fiercest ever heard, he killed the Uk'ten'.

Thunder won, and the boy had helped him [to win]. That is the reason why to this day it thunders [all] around us: we [Thunder and man] are still together. A human being helped him.

Thunder is not fierce, but is very friendly and kind of heart because he knows that it was a little boy who saved him. (But he can become fierce if he does not like something.) He is really very friendly because he knows that it was a human being who saved him.

If the Uk'ten' had overcome Thunder, if Thunder had been shot, I suppose that the Uk'ten' would be lurking about everywhere. I wonder what it would have been like: Thunder would have killed us whenever it thundered, and an Uk'ten' can kill you just by smelling you.

Yan'sa

Thunder and the Uk'ten' (III)

This is the story of when an Uk'ten' and Thunder had a fight. Some people tell it a little bit different. When I hear other people tell it, sometimes it [their version] seems better. This one [version] I know is a little bit similar [to the version of Yan'sa], and others have told it before. The older men used to tell this one [version].[10] This one tells about how the Uk'ten' and Thunder first found each other.

In olden times there were two boys. They used to hunt all the time with bows and arrows. Sometimes they killed birds and squirrels, sometimes rabbits and many [other] smaller animals.

Once the two boys were walking in a deep valley where it was very rugged and rocky. As they were walking among big rocky crags, they found a large snake lying upon a rock. This snake was large enough to eat squirrels. This snake was very lean and hungry. He told the boys to stop, that he wanted to ask them something.

"I'm very hungry," he said to them. "Would you find me some food? I'll eat birds or squirrels. When I become strong again, you can use me, or I'll help you in whatever you are doing in any way that I can for as long as we live."

So the boys decided to help him. The very next morning they brought him birds and squirrels. They brought him food many times, and he was growing stronger and larger.

Several days later they came by and brought him some more squirrels, and this time the snake was huge. Then the boys forgot about him for awhile; but then one day they remembered him.

"Let's go by and see him," they said, "and take him some more birds and squirrels."

When they arrived where the snake was, they called him, and he came out of the rocks. This time he was enormous, and he had grown horns. As he was coming out when they called him, they saw lightning-like sparks before they saw his horns. They gave him his squirrels and birds.

The boys said to him, "You certainly are enormous now! You have grown up!"

The snake said, "Yes, but remember: we are to be friends always." (The snake was duping them because he really wanted to kill them soon.)

The next morning they came nearby. As they entered the valley, they heard some blasts in the valley. After several blasts, the blasts became fainter.

The boys said, "Someone is in trouble over there! Let's hurry and get over there! That's where the snake lives." So they hurried over there.

Soon they saw the snake. This snake that they had fed had coiled himself around something. He and Thunder were fighting. He had enveloped Thunder in his coils. The snake was wound about Thunder so tightly that Thunder could make only faint blasts. Thunder could but barely move.

"Boys! My nephews!"[11] said Thunder. "This snake that is coiled around me is very fierce and kills people. If you can, do something to kill him! Shoot him in the seventh spot. He'll die instantly."

The Uk'ten' cried out, "Don't! Don't! Kill Thunder instead! This Thunder is fiercer [than I]. His blasts will kill you," said the Uk'ten'. (You see, this snake that these boys fed grew up to be an Uk'ten'.)

The boys were undecided what to do.

"Don't you do it! You boys are my grandchildren, and I am

your helper! I always help you! This huge snake that said he would help you was only tricking you. He wanted to kill you. So shoot him on the seventh spot!" said Thunder.

So the boys believed it [the statement of Thunder], and with the Uk'ten' crying, he was shot on the seventh spot. The Uk'ten' fell over, and Thunder was again free.

When Thunder was free, he said to the boys, "Go back in the direction from where you came. On your way build seven fires; build them as you go. You see, the fumes from the Uk'ten' will be stopped by the first fire so that you may have time to build the second fire which then will hold the fumes long enough for you to build the third fire. By the time you build the seventh one, you will be safe—and I will be working for you while you are on your way.

"You can always depend upon me. While we live on earth, or until the world ends, we must protect and help each other," said Thunder. "I am the Ruler of all the fierce things in the world," said Thunder.

So the boys believed it [the statement of Thunder], and they did as they were told to do. They went down into the valley and escaped—so said the very old that lived long ago.

These boys began feeding the small snake, and it grew to be a huge one. There was a small river; there was a deep place in it. That's where he [the snake] was seen after he grew up. He had large horns then, and his horns were shiny and bright; his scales were dazzlingly bright. The boys had devoted a lot of time to feeding him, and he had nearly killed Thunder.

But the boys decided to believe Thunder. That's why Thunder is with us as long as we live. God made it that way: that Lightning-and-Thunder and human beings should live together. Thunder is not dangerous. Some people say that he is. It leads us to believe that they do not think about God when they say such things.

Since we have learned all these things, to invoke the name of Thunder is very useful, and that is the reason that he has helped us. If it hadn't been for that [the assistance given to Thunder by the boys], if they [the boys] had decided to allow the big snake to live, if there were Uk'ten's all over the world, we wouldn't be living—for instance, we [those present] wouldn't be living.

That's all.

Siquanid'

TALES OF MONSTERS

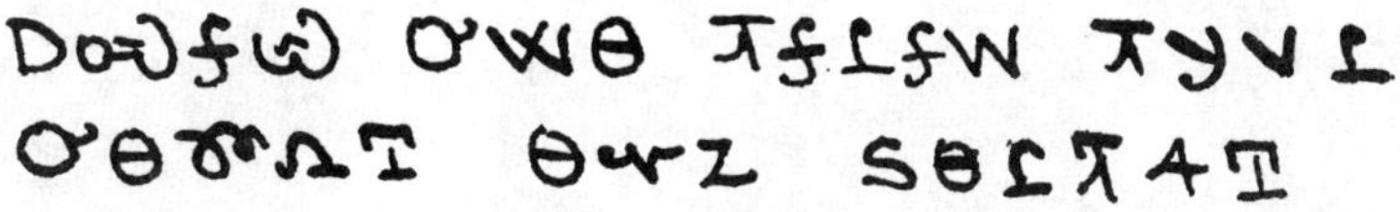

ᎠᏯᏍᎥᏫ ᎤᏪᏇ Ꮏ�F⅃ᏍᏅ ᎿᏴᎥ⅃
ᎤᏇᏉᎥᏔ ᏇᏫᏃ ᏎᏋ⅃ᏔᎯᏔ
" 'The big man has slanting eyes!' they said, and fled."

TALES OF MONSTERS

"THE BIG MAN HAS SLANTING EYES!"

The imagination of Cherokee storytellers appears ever to have been exercised by mythic monsters. Our pantheon of these creatures is admittedly incomplete—(we would especially have liked to recover an account of Awlfinger)—but withal quite representative.

The Tsuhl'gûl' narration we deem to be of outstanding worth, for all its obvious corruption by post-Columbian elements. Yet in some degree all of the monster tales share its quality of reaching back grandly after something lost but not quite forgotten.

Against a Stone Wall

As ubiquitous a figure as there is in Cherokee mythology is that of Nûy'unuw' (the apostrophes represents the vowels "a" and "i," respectively, the famed voiceless phonemes that complicate a language already replete with complexities).[1] The name of the anthropophagous giant Nûy'unuw' is variously rendered into English as: "Stonecoat" in GTEC, HACF, and TDOC; "Stone-shields" in KLOC, which speaks of a race of petrous beings; and "Stone Man" in MMOC.[2] All are inaccurate: Nûy'unuw' means "Stone-clad."

It is a bit surprising that we did not come upon a Stoneclad story. Some of those whom we interviewed readily acknowledged having heard of Stoneclad, but none appeared to be able to reconstruct any sort of narrative about him.

A translation of one of these fascinating but futile interviews is presented here:

In Search of Stoneclad

ASUDI: I haven't heard it [the story of Stoneclad] very accurately. They [presumably the old folk of Asudi's youth] talked of a great many things. One just can't put it [all that they said] into one story because they told so many things.

The coat of this Stoneclad that they told about was very hard. He was difficult to kill. The reason was that his coat was made of stone. He was very large; he wasn't small at all. People were afraid of this large Stoneclad. They didn't want Stoneclad to come near them; they didn't want to attract him. They allowed him to pass by freely.

When God decided to get rid of him, he disappeared, and nobody knows where he went. That's what they say. This Stoneclad disappeared just about that time.[3]

"What became of him?" they asked. "Where did he go? What killed him?" they asked. Nobody knew. It [his disappearance] was just the same as the way other things disappear. As if he went around this [indicating] corner and disappeared, that's the way it was—just as if something passed by, and it disappeared in that direction, and we didn't see it again. We would never know what became of it.

He came and went—that's the way Stoneclad did.

ANNA G. KILPATRICK: What did he look like?

A.: I don't know. They never said what he looked like. He was rather large.

A.G.K.: I suppose he was like a man . . .

A.: I suppose so. He must have been that way.

SIQUANID': Yes, he was.

A.G.K.: He wore this stone coat, didn't he?

A.: Yes. He was not like this little ant called Stoneclad.[4] He was a human being; he was a man. And his clothing was made of stone.

When you hit him, you couldn't hurt him, they said. Regardless of what you used [as a weapon], you couldn't hurt him. But

if we were hit, we would leave just a black streak, or we would be
knocked down. They couldn't hurt him.

S.: That's right.

A.: That's the way he was: he was very strong. He was the
size of a man,[5] this Stoneclad—that's what the old people said.

A.G.K.: Have you heard of anything [in particular] that he
did?

A.: No. I have never heard of him doing anything[6]—only that
he lived alone. Of course, if they had molested him, he could have
done something; but they didn't disturb him. The reason was: they
knew he belonged to God. God had desired him to live, and when
He decided to take him away, He took him away without their
knowing about it.

That's the way it is: just like a man who hasn't been injured,
who hasn't done anything to cause death, if God decides, he can
disappear instantly. Without illness, without pain—exactly the
way it happened [the disappearance of Stoneclad].[7]

That's the way it happened; that's what the old Indians told.[8]

Flint the Terrible

There are truths that defy the statistical apparatus of the so-
ciologist and the comparative powers of the ethnologist. They have
their being in the subjective subtleties of turns of speech, responses
to stimuli, selection of values. One such verity is the fundamentally
Iroquoian material of the Cherokee ethos.

The sheen of the veneer of the Southeast over an intrusive
people has led to some miscalculation as to the thickness of that
outer layer. Affinity, when factors exist such as to permit appraisal,
is clearly perceived and cheerfully confessed by people of both the
Longhouse and the Sacred Fire.[9]

In the myth of Flint (Dawisgûl'), of which we present two
rather wide-ranging variants, one senses a dramatic psychological
shift from the sunlit thought-world of the Southeast to that of
the gray and granitic North.[10] Mooney subsumed Flint to be a

detail leached out of an eroded national cosmology. Such would seem to be the case.

The substitution in the Siquanid' variant of the human trickster-figure Tseg'sgin' for the animal trickster-figure Rabbit as a principal is most easily accounted for by post-Columbian, possibly post-Removal, influence by European folk-sources; but the Tseg'sgin' phenomenon must be thoroughly studied before one can rule out the possibility that the presence of the human-trickster may be due to retention or restoration of an element that existed before the period of Southeastern contact.

The Rabbit Destroys Flint

Flint was the name of a preacher who once lived. He had set a time to do his preaching on top of a mountain.

He told the Rabbit, "This preaching will be on Sunday. I will blow my horn when I am ready to begin."

From the time he got up that [Sunday] morning the Rabbit listened for the horn. By afternoon he still hadn't heard it, so he decided to walk up there [on top of the mountain] and find out what was wrong.

There is no telling how long the preacher had been sleeping, but he was still asleep. The Rabbit got a stick and beat him. Flint flew all to pieces.

Nobody knew what the Rabbit had done because he ran away.[11]

Dalala (N.)

Tseg'sgin' Destroys Flint

We'll talk about Flint the Terrible that lived at one time:

Flint was passing by the house of an old woman. (Flint the Terrible was a very wicked man. He liked to eat people, especially very young children.) Tseg'sgin' was visiting the old woman at her home, they say. When Flint came up to the house, a little boy was playing outdoors. He [Flint] seized the little boy.

The old woman ran crying into the house. She said to Tseg'sgin', "Flint the Terrible has taken away my son! Can't you do something and bring back the child to me alive? If he keeps the child any longer, he will eat him up!" said the old woman.

Tseg'sgin' began to laugh. "I'll kill him," said Tseg'sgin'. "I'll kill that Flint."

The old woman said, "Do anything you can. Just bring back the child alive and as long as we live, I'll do anything you want me to do," said the old woman.

"All right," said Tseg'sgin'.

So he pursued Flint, and far in the distance he caught up with him. When Tseg'sgin' caught up with Flint, he [Flint] seized Tseg'sgin' and said, "I'll take you, too. I'll eat the child first, and I'll finish off with you," Tseg'sgin' was told.

Tseg'sgin' kept saying, "Yes! Good!" as they were walking along. "Eat me just any time you get ready." So while they were walking, Flint grasping Tseg'sgin' by the hand, night come on. They came into a forest.

Flint said, "Now! Let's build a big fire, and we'll sleep here. Early in the morning we'll eat this child. You help me eat him. Then when the sun gets up high, I'll eat you."

Tseg'sgin' said, "All right."

They built the fire. Flint was somewhat restless.[12] The little child nestled close to Tseg'sgin', and Tseg'sgin' began to whittle. He decided to make for himself a big wedge out of wood. He kept working upon it with his knife. He was sitting against a log, and the small child was sitting beside him.

Later on Flint turned around to Tseg'sgin' and said, "What are you making there?"

When Flint said that, Tseg'sgin' said, "I'm making a wedge. I'm going to make it handsome."

"All right," Flint said. "You must give it to me when you finish it." Flint was still restless, and he said, "I'm so very sleepy. I'm going to sleep," Flint said. (He was always sleepy, and he slept very soundly when he slept. Evidently he didn't sleep as lightly as we people.)

So Flint lay down near the fire. Tseg'sgin' kept on whittling his wedge. When he finished his wedge, he made himself a large mallet out of wood. After sleeping awhile, he [Flint] began to snore.

When Tseg'sgin' noticed the snoring, he grasped his wedge and pushed it into Flint. With his wooden mallet, he struck the wedge very lightly. When the wedge was about half-way in, Tseg'sgin' leaped up into the air and hit the wedge as hard as he could. When he did that, Flint burst, and hot flint flew all over that forest.

The Rabbit was sitting nearby in the forest, and when pieces of hot flint hit him, he ran away. He knew of a small tree that had in it a hole in which he thought he might hide. When he put his head into it, his head became fastened. The hole was too small.

He tried to free his head, and his hind legs jumped about wildly. While he was doing that, hot flint was hitting him.

They say that in olden times the Rabbit had seven beautiful tails. This hot flint cut his tails off. They say that there are seven marks where the tails used to be.

That's what the old people who lived long ago said about the Rabbit.

That's all I know.[13]

Siquanid'

The Love Light in Slanting Eyes

The slant-eyed giant Tsuhl'gûl'[14] is designated in MMOC as the Cherokee god of the chase, a statement that one should accept with caution. The aboriginal religion of the Cherokees has not yet been definitively studied. Scholarly investigation in this field, though in some instances of the highest quality, has been of such narrow scope as to preclude the attainment of anything approaching the complete picture; and much that has been accepted as factual betrays the overfacile deduction, the premature conclusion, and the gross error deriving from a lack of knowledge of the language and the ethos of the people.

Information on Tsuhl'gûl'

SIQUANID': . . . Do you know anything about Tsuhl'gûl'?

ASUDI: Did you say Tsuhl'gûl'? Yes. They used to talk . . .

S.: Yes, they used to talk about him. They all had different stories about him, didn't they?

A.: . . . where he lived. He was very wicked, too. People didn't want to live near where he was. He did live, they say.

The older people used to say that he would lean on something and that he was very tall. He used to fall over upon people and mash them. Tsuhl'gûl' was as vicious as the Uk'ten'[15] was. He did a great many things. He was always to be feared.

I have never heard of what became of him other than they said God took him away. What they did to him, or what happened to him, I don't know. I never heard. They just had so many different things to say about him.

A Tale of the Tsunihl'gûl'[16]

This one [story] was told by my father, and he said my grand-mother told it to him:

It was in the Old Cherokee country[17] where these Tsunihl'gûl' lived. They were very tall, huge men.

There was a couple there [in the old Cherokee country], an old man and his wife, who had two daughters of marriageable age. These daughters had heard many times about these tall, huge Tsunihl'gûl'. These daughters were very desirous of seeing [the Tsunihl'gûl'] for themselves because they had heard fantastic tales of these tall, huge men. They had heard that these men could pull up large trees with their bare hands alone. That's what they had heard, and that's what these young women desired to see.

At sunset they would hear a whooping in the west. (In the old Cherokee country there is a great mountain that begins in the east and does not end until it gets to the west.)[18] When he [the whooper] whooped in the west, he whooped four[19] times in tra-versing that mountain. His whooping ceased when he reached the

end of the mountain in the east. At sunset the next evening he
began whooping at the east end of the mountain. He whooped as
he traversed the mountain and ceased [whooping] as he reached
the west end.

It was said that it was a Tsuhl'gûl' who whooped.

"I wonder what we can do to see him," the young women asked
themselves.

So the old man [their father] called in seven conjurers.[20] After
they arrived, they decided to meet for conjuring. So that's what
they did: they [met and] conjured. They determined that an in-
toxicating drink could be made and that they could pour it into
huge cups and place them on the top of the mountain in the path
where he [the Tsuhl'gûl'] would be going.

"He will get drunk from these [cups], and one might be able
to see him because he can't come up the hill" . . . No![21] . . . "When
he gets drunk, we can climb up the mountain and see him, but he
won't be able to see us," said the conjurers.

This liquor that they made was called tsat'.[22] They made it
from corn meal and sugar in those days [!]. So they made this
liquor and put it into big barrels of the sort that hold sixty-four
gallons, and used six of these barrels. They put these barrels in
the path where he would be going. He had a beautiful path: it was
smooth and this [demonstrating] wide.

After they had put the liquor in the middle of the path, they
said, "Now let's listen for him tonight. If he is coming, we can
hear him when he starts. Then we will know what he is going to
do," said the old men. Then they sat in a row outside the house
and looked at the top of the mountain. They watched and listened.

Just at sundown they heard a [first] whoop. The second whoop
came from the very top of the mountain. The third whoop was
from right where the barrels had been put. And the fourth
[whoop] they didn't hear. All was so very silent.

"I wonder what he has done. He has become silent," said the
men [sitting] in a row.

At dawn, when the roosters crowed, they heard him; but he was in the same place [at the barrels].

"Now," they said. "The last whoop came from the same place."

Then in a few minutes he whooped again. Then he whooped a third time in the same place. Several more times he whooped at the same place. He whooped many, many times.

They said, "He is drunk now," because they heard him singing. "So let's climb the mountain, and we will get there [at the barrels] just as it becomes daylight if we go now." So they began climbing the mountain, and they took with them the young women, the women who desired to see the Tsuhl'gûl'.

When they got to the top of the mountain, everything was quiet. Then they heard him whoop right behind them, just out of sight, and they heard another noise, sounding "Daaast'!" The noise was as if he [the Tsuhl'gûl'] were breaking sticks. Then they saw the limbs of trees shaking.

Then they saw the tall, huge man—swaying. In his hand he had a sixty-five[23] barrel, drinking out of it. (It had taken six men to carry one barrel up the mountain, and here he was, holding it in one hand and drinking out of it.) While he was swaying, he was knocking over the smaller trees, and that's what they were hearing. There was a large area over which the Tsuhl'gûl' had flattened the trees while he was drunk. This man that they saw there was whooping, and every few minutes he told himself what a big man he was.

When they came near him, the Tsuhl'gûl' knelt down. He was still taller than they were. Then he lay down and talked with the old men.

Then the young women came up and took a look at his face. They saw that he had slanting eyes, and they fled and said, "He has slanting eyes!"

Then the Tsuhl'gûl' asked the old men if he could have one of the young women: "If you feel like it, will you give me one of the young women?"

"I'll give you both of them," said one of the old men [the father].[24]

So the Tsuhl'gûl' had two young women. The Tsuhl'gûl' was very happy now, and he agreed to go with them [the young women] to their home. They went down the mountain and went home. While going down the mountain, all observed him curiously. The Tsuhl'gûl' was very friendly now.

When they got home, the father wanted to go get some wood [firewood]. The Tsuhl'gûl' said, "I'll go get some wood." He hunted the wood, and found it close by. He used his bare hands to cut the green trees into proper sizes. The in-laws were amazed at his strength.

Later on, there were some neighbors—in those days Tsunihl'-gûl' were fond of women, and even though this Tsuhl'gûl' had two wives, he wanted to marry the neighbors' daughters who lived a mile away—and he visited them often. But when he went to the neighbors' house, if it were still light, he always turned his back away from the people [who lived there]. The Tsuhl'gûl' always told funny stories when he visited these young women. The young women would circle about him, trying to see his face; but the Tsuhl'gûl' would always turn in another direction.

The young women said to each other, "I wonder why he does that—turn away from the light. I wonder what we could do to see him." (The two other young women had already seen him—and they were his wives!)

So the daughters said to each other, "Let's get some sumac to-night and make a fire because it pops [when it burns]. When he turns away, we'll put in our sumac, and the sparks from the popping might alight on him. Then he will turn toward the light."

So before nightfall they gathered a large pile of sumac. Early in the evening the Tsuhl'gûl' arrived. When they gave him a chair by the fire, he sat down and turned away from the fire. When he did that, they put some sumac into the fire. The fire began to burn and to pop, "Das', das', das', das', das', das'!"

A spark fell upon the neck of the Tsuhl'gûl' and the Tsuhl'gûl'
yelled, "Ayô, yô, yô, yô!" He quickly turned around and faced
the blazing fire. The young women saw his eyes: he had slanting
eyes.

"The big man has slanting eyes!" the said, and fled.

When the young women fled, the Tsuhl'gûl' became angry. He
went far away. Then the Tsuhl'gûl' began to conduct himself
riotously and joined a gang [other Tsunihl'gûl'] of roisterers. When
the Tsuhl'gûl' joined this group, God permitted them all to live
among people like us [of normal size]; but they were always
taking all the women and wives away from ordinary-sized men
until smaller men were without women. (The Tsunihl'gûl' were
very wicked, but women liked them.)

So God declared that this was not the place for Tsunihl'gûl'.
God decided to send them all to the west, to the end of the world,
and that's where they live now. Someday they may return, and
we will see them, they say.

This is just the length that this story is. This is all I know about
how Tsunihl'gûl' lived.

Siquanid'

Magic Is Wherever You Find It

The Creek, Alabamas, and Koasatis[25] also told, or perhaps still
tell, a tale that is fundamentally the same as the one here that
Yan'sa told us one evening by kerosene lamplight in his century-
old log cabin situated within sight and sound of a paved highway
busy with those traveling in another age.

The Giant Lizard

Now I'll tell you another one [story], though. This was also
told long ago. This happened in a forest on a very high hill where
people used to go—and when a person went there, he disappeared,
gone forever.

Now once there were three men walking there in that forest

on that hill. They saw something astounding: a huge and tall stump that used to be a tree; they saw that the ground was very smooth around this stump and that there were bones all around it.

One of the three [men] became bold. We wanted to know what was in the stump, and he climbed up there [to the top of it]. When he reached the top of the stump, he looked down, and there right below him [in the hollow of the stump] was a giant lizard!

He [the man] gave himself up for lost. To the other two [men] standing below he said, "Run off and get away from this [animal?]! As for me, there's nothing I can do!"

The lizard was clever. He came out and said to himself, "This man up there can't get away from me," and then he leaped to the ground.

But he chased those two [men] that were running away from him. Within just a short distance he caught one of them. He brought him back and laid him down by the tree [i.e., stump]. The other [first] man was slowly climbing down. Now he chased the third one [man] and finally caught him.

Now the one [man] that climbed down ran off in a different direction. The lizard brought in the second man that he had caught and laid him down by the tree [stump]; then he chased the man who had climbed down and had run in a different direction.

But the man reached where people were, and he told them about this lizard that was chasing him. They tried to shoot him [the lizard], but the bullet slid along his back. But when he got very near, he opened his mouth wide. They shot him in the mouth with their guns, and when they shot him in the mouth, he died.

There was something magic about him. In his jaw were dry brown spots. These Indians[26] took them out. These Indians were grateful for the supernatural help that they [the dry, brown spots] would always give. These were to be used just like the scales of an Uk'ten',[27] to help them [the Indians]. These brown spots that came from the jaw of the lizard were called uwôd'.

Yan'sa

The Touchy Turtle and His Waspish Wife

The following story is a rather curious synthesis of at least these four motifs far-flung over the Southeastern cultural area: (1) the enormous bird of prey; (2) the sagittary turtle; (3) the pouting turtle; (4) the turtle as poor provider, with resultant rupture of conjugal peace.

The Tlaniqu' (written in the Sequoyah syllabary Tla-ni-qua but usually pronounced with the final vowel silent) is discussed at some length in MMOC and is memorialized by a number of place names in the "Old Cherokee country." The community of Fairfield, a couple of miles or so northeast of Stilwell in Adair County, is known to the Cherokees as Tlanuwôh', a dialectal form of this word, but as yet we do not know why.

The Tlaniqu' and the Turtle

This one [story] was told long ago. There was an old man who used to tell us of many things. His name was Tsali Udisûdiyet'. Some people called him Tsali Uwôse.[28] He used to live at Barber.[29] He used to tell all the time about olden things, and he told this one [story]:

Long, long ago creatures that lived in the woods—creatures that had four legs, that had wings, and also creatures that crawled upon the ground—all these creatures were molested by a huge bird that existed called the Tlaniqu'. There were many of these large birds, and they ate all these creatures that lived in the woods.

Once there was a cub playing out in the open where they had cleared [a space] where they [cubs] could play. One day there must have been three or four of the cubs playing in a circle when a Tlaniqu' swooped down right in the middle of them and carried off one of the cubs.

They [the woods-creatures] all went forth to find out how they could kill the bird. At first he was flying around low, carrying the cub, but he kept getting higher. They [the woods-creatures] went all over the village (they had a huge village in the woods) inquiring around as to how they could kill that bird, the bird that had taken away the baby bear. The bird kept getting higher and higher until he was so high one couldn't see him. When they looked up there, they could just barely see his shadow.

This creature they called the Turtle was sitting somewhere. They didn't consider him to be a very intelligent creature; they didn't think he had very good sense. He didn't talk very much.

"Go ask him. He might be able to do something about it [the situation]. He might think of a way to kill him [the Tlaniqu'],") they said. So they all ran over to where he was sitting. He was sitting there whittling. When they got close to him, they observed that he was whittling a very small stick and that he was using a very sharp knife. He kept on whittling.

They asked him, "Could you do something for us? The big fierce flying bird, the Tlaniqu', has stolen one of our cubs. You see, he is flying away up in the air right now; and if you can kill him, if you can do that, we will do for you whatever you want us to do for as long as we live. Or we will help you if you need anything in the way of making a living if you will just let us know," all the wild animals told him.

So the Turtle believed it [what he was promised]. He said, "I believe I can kill him. But there is one thing [to consider]: I am very slow in getting ready. If you don't mind waiting on me, I can kill him," said the Turtle as he spoke.

So all the animals told him, "All right, go ahead and get ready. When you get ready, you let us know how we can help you."

So he began to whittle out a bow. After a time, when they thought he might have finished it, they went to see him. They said to the Turtle, "Have you finished your bow now?"

The Turtle said, "I still need to do a little more."

They were running about crying, and they said, "The bird will return and get the second one [cub]!"

They all feared this very large Tlaniqu'. He [the species] was a fierce bird, and later on he ate human beings when human beings came to live upon the earth. But at this time there were only talking animals [in existence]. It was much longer ago than when this happened [the advent of man] when this bird was eating such wild animals as bears, wolves, and deer. He used to get them—that's what used to happen.

Then the animals came the second time to see the Turtle and go ask him if he were finished with the bow. When they asked him, he said, "Yes, I have just finished. But I still have to string the bow." He was working upon a skin, cutting it for a string. "When I get enough cut, I'm going to wind it at the end."

The animals were very restless as they looked up into the sky and saw the bird still carrying the cub. "Maybe he's finished now," they said. "Let's go ask him." So they all ran over and asked the Turtle.

"I'm putting my string on now," said the Turtle.

"Well, now he's nearly finished with the bow," they said as they all gathered about. Now again they said, "Go ask him if he is finished now," and they said, "Are you finished?"

"I still need to cut my arrow," he said.

Then they waited again. They were very restless. They moved about all the time while they were watching this bird carrying the cub. Then they said, "Let's go ask him if he is finished now," and they all went to him again. So they asked him, "Are you finished this time?" they asked him.

"Yes, I'm finished now, but there is this in which you will have to help me: When you help me, I want you to place my foot upon the bow, and when I get hold of the bow, then you must make my arrow straight. You must point my arrow directly at the bird, and when I pull the bow and shoot it, the arrow will fly straight to the bird, and the bird will fall."

So they all did all that they could, and the Turtle turned over on his back, and they made his arrow straight. The Turtle placed his back leg against the bow, and then he pulled the string to let the arrow fly. When he pulled it, he let go, and when the arrow was loosed, it flew into the air and hit the Tlaniqu' right in the middle of the heart, and he [the Tlaniqu'] fell, turning over and over as he fell.

When he fell to the ground, the group fell upon him. They all clutched at him as he flopped about. The Turtle spoke up and said, "Now don't you break my bow! I like it very much."

One of the elderly animals stood up and said, "I'll make them stop!" But they all were in a furious scramble with this bird. The elder said, "Don't you break that bow! Don't you break that bow! You'll break it for him! Don't go at things so wildly. The bird is dead anyhow."

But they didn't obey the oldster and kept on. They kept on beating this bird, and they broke the bow all to pieces.

So the Turtle was very angry because this bow was the best that he had ever made, and he liked it very much. That's why in his heart he was very angry about the bow. He was angry!

Then the various animals considered what to do with the Tlaniqu'. "What shall we do with him? Shall we divide him up?"

"Yes. We will divide him after we take his feathers off and his insides out. We will cut the meat all up and divide it."

The Chief said, "Now let's give the choice piece to the Turtle."

When he said that, they went to ask the Turtle, "What part is your favorite piece of meat of that sort, from a flying bird? We want to cut you the part you like best."

"No part of it. I don't like any part of it," said the Turtle.

One of them said, "The back usually has the best meat on it. Go ask the Turtle if he likes the back."

"Would you like the back piece, Turtle?" they asked him.

"I don't want any," said the Turtle. He spoke in an angry voice.

"Would you like the liver?" they asked him.

"No," he said. "I don't want it. That would make me sick."

"Well, would you like the heart?"

"No. I don't want to be heart-sick."

Then they gave up, and when they gave up, they said, "You must say what part you like best."

"I just don't want any part of it," he said. "I would have liked one thing: that you had not broken my bow. You see, I had worked very hard to make it, but you have destroyed it," he said when the Turtle did speak.

They were very sad when they heard him say that.

The Turtle had a wife, and she was at home waiting for him, hoping that he would bring something to eat so that she could feed the very large family.

After they [the woods-creatures] had divided up all the meat, all that was left was a large clot of blood. So the Turtle went to the spot [where the meat had been divided] and found some blood on leaves. Then he wrapped this blood up in the leaves, and the more he wrapped, the larger it [the package] became.

So he took this package of blood to his wife. When he arrived home, he was carrying a huge package upon his back.

His wife thought, "He carries a lot of things on his back."

He said to his wife, "Unwrap it."

So she began to unwrap it. After a while she had leaves all around her.

"Where is it?" she said.

He said, "It's underneath. Unwrap some more."

She kept on unwrapping, and she was at the point of giving up because she had such a large pile of leaves around her. Then she found that small clot of blood wrapped up in one little leaf. That's what the Turtle had been given [for his share of the Tlaniqu'].

When his wife finally unwrapped this [package], she found just one small clot of blood on one little leaf.[30]

"You certainly have a small mind!" she told the Turtle. "You know how many we have to feed—and look at what you brought us!" she said. "And look at what a huge bird you killed! It looks as if you would have brought your family a good piece of meat!" said the angry wife to the Turtle.

She threw this leaf and blood in his face, and it [the blood] blinded his eyes. They say that's the reason why the Turtle has red eyes. He was blinded by the blood of the Tlaniqu'. His wife was the one who blinded him with the blood-clot. The blood of the Tlaniqu' spattered into his eyes. That's the reason he has red eyes, said the old people who lived long ago.

The Turtle had become very angry because they [the woods-creatures] had broken his bow. That's the reason why even to this day he still becomes angry easily and snaps at you. He is still angry about the bow that had been broken.

That's what was said by the people who lived a long time ago. That's all about the Turtle.

Siquanid'

THE LITTLE PEOPLE

ӨᎪᏩᏃ ᏦᏋᏒ ᏴᎾ ᎾᏃ ᏴᎾ ᏵᎾᏬᎧᏔ
ᏂᎪᎪᎭᎢ ᏠᎾᏘᎠᎹᏐ ᏦᏋᏌᎢ

"But in those days human beings and the Little People associated with each other."

THE LITTLE PEOPLE

THE LEPRECHAUNS OF OKLAHOMA

Since the authors consider this book to be essentially a collection of source materials, it would seemingly suffice merely to call attention to the fact that the Cherokees subsume several classes of Little People, each of which possesses distinctive attributes. This would also seem to be the place to point out that the white people who have some familiarity with Cherokee culture have a distressing tendency to confound the anthropoid Little People with the spirit animals, but are nevertheless in possession of a sizable body of tales that, although secondhand, are well worth the collecting and the preserving.

A Small Cloud of Witnesses

We have extracted from our tapes a sheaf of anecdotes relating to encounters with the Little People either by persons known to the narrator or, in one case, by the narrator herself. It almost goes without saying that each of these little tales was related to us without the slightest trace of incredulity upon the part of the speaker. To the average Cherokee with some degree of traditional upbringing, the existence of the Little People is an indisputable fact, and if he has himself been denied contact with them, he is almost certain to be acquainted with someone who has enjoyed the privilege.

The Oklahoma Cherokees do not appear to believe that anything untoward is likely to accrue from seeing, or even conversing with, the Little People. But although they are benign, there is a danger of becoming fascinated by them and following them off to unpredictable adventures.

The Little People of Standing Rock[1]

I know of things I heard about that were in the Cherokee
country a long time ago—long, long ago: the salines for instance.
Over there where the dam is,[2] where the great lake [Tenkiller] is
located, there used to be springs that they called "Salt Springs."
These springs were beyond what they used to call *Old Cookson
Hills.*[3]

There were some people who worked there. There were two
men who were neighbors who worked there. The name of one was
Ig'[4] and the name of the other was Ogan'.[5]

They went to work there, and when they finished work, they
started home. The road was quite near Nûya Digadôga.[6] There was
a place where Adeyôh'[7] used to live, and that's where one had to
go downhill to the old road, and that's where they were walking
when night fell.

They lost their way. They both were hunting the road, and in
hunting the road they lost each other and neither one knew which
way to go.

Ig' reached the bank of a creek. As he looked down into the
water, away down into deep water, he saw some people. There was
a house down there in the deep water. He saw people down there
in the house.

When he moved away from the bank, he went to a rocky area.
There was a door there, and he entered it. When he went in, he discovered that he was in the same room into which he had looked.

When he went into that room, he found many people in there.
They were Little People, and they were dancing. There were old
folk in there, too, but they were also small.

They all [Ig' and his hosts] conversed a little bit, then they
[the Little People] offered him food. They gave him raccoon meat
to eat. When he finished eating the raccoon, they cleared off the
scraps and put them in a barrel which was placed near the fireplace. Then afterwhile when they took the lid off the barrel, a
live raccoon emerged. He [Ig'] thought he had eaten that raccoon.

They opened the door for the raccoon, and it walked through it.

All night the Little People danced, but this man just sat near a very old man who was sitting upon the barrel and watched them. The old man who was sitting upon the barrel was toying with dried beeswax, poking it with his cane.

That's the way it [the situation] was until morning, at which time he left. He went out the door, and after he had walked a short distance, he looked back, but he could not see the door. It had disappeared.

He went up the hill just a little way and found his friend Ogan'. They [the two friends] didn't know it, but they had been near each other all the while. Ogan' had had a similar experience.

It was amazing what they saw—and I think that there are Little People still in the world today. Some people call them Anigûnehiyat'.[8]

This story is not very old because it happened in this area.[9]

That's all.

Yan'sa

Yûn'wulôs' and the Little People

There was a man named Yûn'wulôs'.[10] This Yûn'wulôs' Wôyi[11] was an elderly man. I used to live near him, and I have lived with him. This story that I am going to tell was told to me by Yûn'wulôs' Wôyi while we were walking in the woods.

Where the dam is today, there was a large valley there where they did a lot of fishing.

They [a fishing party] had gone down in that valley one night to fish, and they decided to sleep [there]. About midnight Yûn'wulôs' woke up. A huge rock had rolled down from the top of the hill. He became frightened, arose, and looked in that direction [from whence the disturbance had come]. Next he heard some talking. As they [who were talking] were passing by [along the top of the hill], they were saying, "There are quite a few fishermen sleeping tonight." He [Yûn'wulôs'] could hear their footsteps.

After a while he saw a light, and he decided that they were carrying a lantern.

Right west of where the dam is, at one time were large bluffs. That's where he heard the voices and saw the light.[12]

This story that I'm telling took place a long time ago. It happened when Yûn'wulôs' was a young man. This wasn't all.[13] They say that there have been Little People long before this [when Yûn'wulôs' was a young man].

That's all.

Siquanid'

Uwedasat' and the Little People

I'll tell you this short one [story]. This was told to me by Uwedasat'.[14]

He said that in the valley near his home there was a deep hole, and that is where these People with magic powers lived. "I sometimes go there," he used to say. "We used to get together," he told me. "They have a beautiful place [to live]. They used to have dances with music. Sometimes I used to pass there at night, and they were dancing, and I could hear beautiful music. Sometimes I would just pass by, and at other times I would join them," the old man used to say.

Siquanid'

The Little Person of Sugar Mountain

My father told me this [story]:

He said that he and his grandmother lived together over there at Sugar Mountain[15] over there across Caney Creek.[16] About two miles from where I live on the road is called Sugar Mountain.

At one time (my grandmother said my father had told her) when water was scarce, about halfway up Sugar Mountain was a spot that was always damp, as if there were a spring there—she said he used to say.[17] My grandmother dug out the place.

"It was very soft digging," said my father who was a boy at the time. "I was playing around nearby while my grandmother was digging, hoping there would be some water there," he said. "So after a while, when she had dug as far as her arm could reach, water gushed out, and it overflowed [the excavation]; and when she put her hand in again to scoop out the soil, I heard some whooping," my father said. "The whoop was very loud. There was a boy named Ugalôg',[18] the son of Kôdesg"[19] who lived there [nearby]. We used to whoop at each other often in the past," said my father.

" 'Ugalôg' is whooping at you. Whoop back at him,' my grandmother said to me," he said. "But when I at last decided where it [the whooping] was coming from, [I decided that] it was from the hole where the water was coming from," my father used to say, "and I told my grandmother that it was not Ugalôg' who was whooping, but 'it is down where you are sticking your hand in, that's where the whooping is coming from,' I told her," said my late father. "When my grandmother listened, she decided it was coming from the hole, and she said, 'Yes, it is a little Person[20] who is whooping,' she said. 'Let's leave!' So we ran away," my late father said. "Finally we arrived home," he said.

And that's the way it was in those days. Those events were related to me by these two persons [Uwedasat'[21] and his father], and I thought I would give you these short accounts.

People say that Uwedasat' had magic powers. They used to say that he could predict the future very quickly [?].

That's all I know. That's all.

Siquanid'

An Encounter with the Little People

We made plans to go fishing, and when we started, we went down this [indicating] road. We went some distance where there was a deep pool [in the creek], and that's where we fished.

One of the young boys that went with us kept looking back in the direction from which we had come. I was sitting here [indicating in the middle], the boy was sitting here [indicating to one side], and the other person here [indicating to the other side].

I didn't see anything, but the boy kept looking back. After the boy had turned around several times, I turned around and looked, and I saw three people just this high [indicating about three feet] standing there. Two were women, for they had on dresses; one was a man, for he had on a pair of pants. The man had his hand on a tree. I'm sure the tree is still there.

I kept turning to watch them. Then the second time I looked, they had started walking in that [indicating] direction into the woods.

The boy stopped turning around then, and when we got home, I asked him why he had been looking back so much. He said, "There was somebody behind us talking, and when I turned, I didn't see anybody. Then I would hear them talking again."

I told him that there were three persons looking at us from behind us. The boy didn't say anything. He didn't say whether he saw anything or not. He was silent.

That's all.

Gahnô

Deer Love

"A Tale of the Deer People" bears a strong resemblance to both a Hichiti (p. 91) and a Koasati (p. 193) story in SMTS, a weak resemblance to an Alabama (p. 126) narrative in the same collection, a Choctaw story in BCBL (p. 32), a Chitimacha example in DSSA (p. 14), and a Biloxi one in DSOB (pp. 83-84); but all these pale beside the richness of imagery, opulence of detail, and psychological depth with which Siquanid' imbues his account.

A Tale of the Deer People

Long ago there were two young men. They were brothers. They had never before taken any notice of young women. These two boys were handsome, and they used to like to go to the stomp dances.[22]

When they went to these dances and stayed all night, there were other people there that they didn't know. These people were strangers; most of them were women.

Two of the women wore all-black, shiny clothes. They wore matching gloves that were long and beautiful. These women were beautiful. As soon as the dance was over, these women would disappear, and when the dance started again, they would run in from another direction and join the dance.

As the women did these things, the young men watched them. One of the young men said to his brother, "I'm going to find out where these women come from. I'm going to ask one of them."

"All right," his brother answered, "and if you can go with them, I'll just wait around here until you return."

"Good."

It was just at dawn, when it becomes light, that the young man joined the dance and was dancing between the young women as they were stomp-dancing. So the young man asked one of the women, "Where do you come from? I see you come to the dance often."

So the woman turned around and said, "We live just right over there, not very far from here, on the other side of the creek."

"When are you going home?" asked the young man.

"We are leaving soon. We will soon get ready to go."

One of the women questioned him and said, "Are you going with us?"

"Yes, I'll go with you," said the young man.

"If you will go ahead on the way we are going, you can be waiting for us at the creek. When we arrive, we all wash our faces and then go across to the other side," said the young women. The young women liked him very much. These beautiful young women were human beings.[23]

He waited for them at the creek, and sure enough, as it was getting light, they arrived. They [the young women] went down the hill to the creek and washed their faces; so did the young man.

After they [all] washed their faces, they walked in single file in a very narrow, smooth path. It was very rocky all around them. It looked as if there were a mountain [upon which they were walking?] made of stone. They walked along a bluff a long way, and then afterwhile one of the young women said, "Here it is."

So they stopped, and it was rocky there. When they stopped there, one of the young women opened a stone door, and when they had entered, she closed the door.

After they entered, he noticed that everything was just the same as it was on the outside. He noticed that there were many people there, all kinds. They were having some kind of meeting. They were going to have a feast. They were cooking all sorts of wild animal meat. They had beautiful tables.

The young man stood and gazed at these activities. He saw sitting in a corner an old man with a long white beard. The young man moved near the old man.

"You did an amazing thing in that you were able to follow the young women," said the old man to the young man. "I have told everybody that they did well for themselves. They found themselves a young man," said the old man.

"Yes, I came with them," said the young man.

"We will have good things to eat afterwhile, but we are going to have a ball game first," said the old man.

So they had this game with the ball-sticks.[24] After the ball game was over, a very long table loaded with food was ready, and cooking was still going on. Some of these people that were cooking, he had never seen before, and some of the dead were there cooking. They were cooking in a huge pot.

After eating, the young man went back and resumed talking to the old man. The old man said to the young man, "Tomorrow there is going to be a race, and if you'd like to do so, you can enter the race. Those two young women that you brought in here, they both can be yours if you win," said the old man. "There will be seven places [goals] to run to, and when you arrive at the seventh place, you will have won, and I will give you the young women," said the old man.

"All right," said the young man. "I didn't bring my racing clothes. I suppose I need to wear those," said the young man.

"Yes," the old man said. "I have beautiful racing clothes that I wear when I race. And I will let you wear them," said the old man.

So the next morning they made ready [for the race]. The young man put on the racing clothes in a room where he was allowed to change his clothes. When he put on these clothes, he was dressed from head to toe in beautiful shiny clothes, and his hands were covered with beautiful gloves. As he was looking at his hands and feet, he noticed that they had become like the feet of a deer. He was amazed at how beautiful he appeared.

When it was nearly time for the race, the old man said to the young man, "Now you are just about ready to race."

The old man snapped his whip to signify that it was time to race, and as he did that, the two young women appeared at the sides of the young man, and they ran with him down the wide road. The three disappeared [from view] as they ran upon that smooth road. The young man had on a hat that had a lot of horns on it, and it disappeared from view.

After they had run awhile, they saw another person, dressed just as he [the young man] was dressed, a little smaller in size, running down the road coming toward them. They [the young man and the stranger] met face to face in the middle of the road. When they met face to face, they butted each other, and the smaller man reeled back in the road; but he arose, and they butted again, and they butted each other seven times. On the seventh butt the smaller one [man] was vanquished.

The young man and the young women continued running down the road. Down the road they met another one [man]. This time he [the stranger] had huge antlers. They [the young man and the stranger] butted seven times, and on the seventh time the young

man won. They [the young man and the young women] met a
third one [man]. He [the young man] defeated the third one.

So he [the young man] and the young women continued running. The one [man] he [the young] man met on the sixth encounter was a little larger [than the others]. They [the young
man and the stranger] butted much longer upon this occasion,
but still the young man won.

After starting for the seventh time, the young man and the
young women continued running with the young man in the
middle until they met the seventh [man]. This seventh one was
almost all black, with little white spots, and he had huge antlers.
They [the young man and the stranger] fought for a long, long
time, and after the young man was butted the seventh time, he
lost.

So the young man returned; and the winner, the huge black
one, took the two girls away. He [the young man] returned to
the old man and said, "I have lost." Afterwhile the two young
women returned, and when they changed their clothes, they became human again.

This old man was not just an ordinary human being: he was
more powerful. He was Thunder.[25] While the young man was
running, this man Thunder was helping him to be stronger with
his thunder and lightning. That was the reason why the old man
remained at the starting-place: he was conjuring the big-horned
deer that were fighting the young man. The reason that the young
man lost was that it was not yet time for him to have a young
woman.[26]

When he returned to the old man, he changed his clothes and
he became an ordinary man again. The young man said, "I suppose
I'll leave now."

But the young women didn't want him to go. "Stay with us a
little while longer," they said. So he remained quite a while with
them, and they [all] visited about near the place. They visited the
various activities that were going on.

(These young women were young Little People. These Little People can change themselves into other creatures. If they say, "Let me be like this," they can change themselves into creatures that live in the woods. That's the way it was then [at the time of the story].)

Then he [the young man] returned home, which was very near where the stomp dances took place. When he went home, the two young women took him, and they took him as far as where they had first met him, at the stomp dance. There was a stomp dance going on when they arrived there. At this dance there were real people only; and when they arrived there, he saw his brother.

"Where did you go? You were so long!" his brother asked.

"I can't tell you how far I went. I was with these young women who dance here a very long time," he said.

His brother asked, "What was it like where you went?"

"Well, there is so much to tell that one cannot tell it all. You see, I entered a race, and I was told that if I won it, I could have both of these young women," said he. "But, you see, I lost. You see, when we fought, I was beaten upon the seventh encounter. That's the reason why they have brought me back. I wouldn't have returned had I won."

"Well, well,"²⁷ he [the other brother] said.

When the dance was over, they returned home together. They lived with their grandmother.

Their grandmother said, "Where have you been? You've been gone so long!"

"Just out there visiting around," he [the brother who had had the foregoing experiences] said.

"Well, what were you doing?" she said.

"I was visiting at somebody's house," he said.

He became ill from thinking about these young women: they made him ill. Every day he grew weaker. He thought only of how the women looked. They [his family] made him a bed out on the porch because he was growing so ill. He became very weak, too weak to be moved about. As he lay upon his bed upon the porch, he had his pillow folded so that he was in a sitting position, and he could look around him and could see the path that went down the hill to the spring.

While his grandmother was attending him, sitting close by, the young man kept gazing toward the path. Afterwhile a beautiful young woman with two children appeared from that direction. The children that she had with her were beautiful. They were a boy and a girl. The energetic children saw him as he lay upon his pillow, ran to him, and cried, "Father! Father! Father!" and romped all over him. When the young woman came up, she began to attend him.

The grandmother thought to herself, "He never had a woman friend . . . I didn't know that there was a woman that he had been courting . . . ," the grandmother thought.

About the third day the young woman decided to go get some water and took a bucket down to the spring. When she went to get the water, the children followed her. (No, that's not true! The children remained and kept on playing near their father. He WAS their father, wasn't he?)

The grandmother was still astounded at what she was seeing. When the young woman went to get the water, the grandmother decided that this was her opportunity to question him about her; so she asked him, "Where did this beautiful woman that you have been courting live? I didn't know [of the liaison], so I am amazed. You see, we don't have such beautiful women in this vicinity, and those that come from away off are not as beautiful as she is," she told him.

"Yes, that's true," he said. "You see, I went to a place where I had never been before, and I was with two women there, and this is one of them."

As he said that, the young woman was coming up the hill, and she heard him. She dropped her bucket and began to run. The little children followed her, and they [all] had gone but a little way when they changed into deer, a doe and two fawns. They disappeared into the forest.

This was told a long time ago by the old people who were living then. That's what happened in those days. The conjurers followed [and observed] the Little People. That's why they could see such strange things happen.

They say that there is another world just like this under this one, but we can't go there. But in those days human beings and the Little People associated with each other. That's what happened to this young man, they say.

That's all I know.

Siquanid'

Inside Information

Quite a few of the Eastern Cherokee incantations that have been translated and made available to inspection through publication[28] deal with attracting or retaining the affection of someone of the opposite sex, or with the nullification of the charms of a rival. To the best of our knowledge, no parallel study has ever been made among the Oklahoma division of the tribe.

The language of these charms, bristling with the most formidable of archaisms, sometimes rises to towering poetic heights, but is also sometimes all but unintelligible to the laity.

We have here two tales of love charms obtained directly from the supernatural source.

The Little Person and the Hunter

These people that lived long ago called the Little People were very powerful. They say that they could transform themselves into other [human] people. They had only to see a person that they wanted to be, and they could change themselves into that person. If we saw them, and they saw us, they could transform themselves into us. They say that Little People are very much like real people.[29] The women are beautiful with long hair.

Once upon a time there was a young man who was a hunter. While this young man was sitting in the shade, watching for squirrels, he heard some singing away down in the valley. When he heard this singing, he turned and looked all around him, but he didn't see anyone. He saw a grapevine swinging and kept hearing the singing. He wanted to see who was doing it [causing the grapevine to swing and doing the singing]. Finally, much later, he saw a small man sitting upon the grapevine. He was grasping the grapevine and singing.

Now this is that this Little Person said as he sang:

Yû- wu- sti- i   nû- dô- gû- hnô

i- ya nû- da- qua-   du- yû- hnû- hi

tsi- ne- gô si-   yu a- yû

ga- gô- ke- hnô   na- squô na- sgi

i- ni- ga- yô- hi   ya- qua- le- hne- hô

a- yû di- nô-   si di- na- ga- li-

sgû- quô wa- gi- gi- sû a- qua- tsa- nû- gi

u- hi- sô- ti[30] ni- ge- sû- na. Di- gi- di- di- di.[31]

(Onomatopoeia of footsteps)

That's what the Little Person said when he sang.

The young squirrel hunter was told to sit down and learn this song. "You must say this whenever there is a young woman who is indifferent toward you. You must sing this song that I have sung for you, and you must think of the young woman's name. Early in the morning when the sun comes up, when it is very large and red, you must face the sun and sing the song. You can't fail to get the woman you want, if you will sing this song that I have taught you"—that is what the squirrel hunter was told. That's how the hunter learned that these Little People were so powerful.

If we but see them, they can bewitch us, and all the more so if they have just sung this song. That's what happened to this young hunter: he was put under an enchantment. He saw the one [the supernatural being] that he desired to see. That [to be an enchanter himself] was what he was taught to do.

All the adults after his time taught this same magic to the young folk. All the young folk began to work this magic on each other. Much later they lost this magic. The older folk said that the Little People caused them to forget the magic, that the Little People took it back.

My father told me that. Tsali Usgasit'[32] was my father.

That's all I know.

One can tell very interesting things about these Little People that were told by our forefathers. These Little People were very anik'tahna.[33]

Siquanid'

Tsugûtsalala[34]

There was something that could fly that was very much like Little People called Tsugûtsalala, which was a bird. This bird whose name was Tsugûtsalala was beautiful in appearance. It was speckled like a quail, but much more beautiful than a quail. You had but to see it, and it could bewitch you. It also sang.

Somewhere a young man who was inebriated was walking near a fence. At that time the poke-salad berries were ripening and poke-salad[35] usually grows up against fences. Tsugûtsalala was sitting upon these poke-salad plants, and he had eaten too many [berries].

The young man who was walking heard someone singing. He went directly to the poke-salad patch to find out who was singing. He saw a small bird sitting there singing its own name, "Tsugûtsalala."

So it [the bird] bewitched the young man. He stood there and looked at it quite a while, he said as he told about it. The young man sat down after he heard the singing and looked at Tsugûtsalala. The old people had told him what the bird looked like, and he knew what it was.

So now he had an opportunity to see it, this bird called Tsugûtsalala, and when he saw it, he was bewitched because he had heard the singing. So when he heard the singing, he learned the song. The bird was singing his song by saying his own name, "Tsugûtsalala." This is what he was saying when he was singing:

de- ga- le- hne- e- hô   u- tlô- hie- dlû- i-

dû- hnû- se squû- le-   ne- e- hô.³⁶

That's what he said when he sang.

U- na- kô- la- ti   gi- ga- ge-   quu

i- gô- quô- du- u-   hi   dô- ti- qua- la- sgû

gu- wa- dû- hnû- û- hi   i- gû- quô- du- u- hi.³⁷

That's how Tsugûtsalala sang, said the older people of long ago, and that's what was told to me. I suppose it is true because it [Tsugûtsalala] bewitched the young man.

"You must sing this, if there is ever a young woman you want to marry and you won't fail to get her," he was told.

That's what he was told, they [the older people] said. He was given something to make himself supernaturally more attractive, they said when they told me.

That's all I know.

Siquanid'

TSEG'SGIN' STORIES

ᏤᎩᏍᎩᏂ ᎤᏣᏔ ᎠᏓᏅᏖᏔ ᎨᏎ

"Tseg'sgin' was exceedingly clever."

TSEG'SGIN' STORIES

JACK THE DEVIL

It would be a convenience to assume that Tseg'sgin' is a survival or transference of some mythological trickster-hero now unidentifiable, but we sincerely do not believe this to be the case. In the first place, there is no record, written or oral, attesting to the existence of any such figure; and in the second place, all the Tseg'sgin' stories possess built-in features that are either European, post-contact, or both.

The Negro Jack (or John) fulfils many of the requirements for having been the prototype of Tseg'sgin' (see HMAM, passim). He, too, is a sharper getting ahead by his wits, occasionally besting even Satan himself. But he lacks certain qualities of stupidity and ridiculousness. There is nothing in the Cherokees' Tseg'sgin' of the folk-hero who wins from a position of weakness. Essentially he is unlovable, reprehensible, basically dull. He lucks into some of his greatest victories.

There is a similarity too obvious to disregard between the two words Tseg'sin', Jackson, and Tseg'sgin', "Jack the Devil." To this day among the conservatives where one finds Tseg'sgin' stories being exchanged, the name of Andrew Jackson, the man who repaid Cherokee friendship and valor at Horseshoe Bend with the horrors of the Trail of Tears, is the symbol of trickery and deceit and of opportunism at the expense of others.

Falling for an Old Trick

The motif of an individual who wins a race by digging a pit for his opponent is not an un-Indian touch, nor is the racehorse as foreign a cultural element as it may seem. A certain social class

99

of nineteenth-century Cherokees were noted breeders of blooded horses and devotees of the racecourse.

Tseg'sgin' Has a Race

Tseg'sgin' has a racehorse. There was a rich [white?] man who also had a racehorse. They [Tseg'sgin' and the rich man] agreed to have a race and bet on it.

When the day for the race came, Tseg'sgin' dug a hole in the road over which they were going to race. He dug the hole very deep.

When they raced, the rich man fell into the hole, and Tseg'sgin' ran on and won the race.

That's all.

Dalala (N.)

Tseg'sgin'[1] Races the Chief[2]

Tseg'sgin' was exceedingly clever. He won out even over a Chief. He began by making noises outdoors, annoying him [the Chief] at night. The Chief recognized Tseg'sgin'.

One evening the Chief said, "I know you, Tseg'sgin'! Let's meet in the morning and have a contest," he was told. They were to be on horses. They selected a spot on the road for a meeting place. Tseg'sgin' selected a very ugly horse.

When morning came, he saddled up the horse. He decorated the saddle with strips of rags. He took his gun, mounted the horse, and went to meet the Chief. The Chief was there waiting. When the Chief's handsome horse saw the unsightly horse of Tseg'sgin', he became frightened, tried to run away—and did.

Tseg'sgin' chased after him [the Chief] and asked why he was running away. But you see the Chief's horse was running away from Tseg'sgin' 's horse because of fright. That was the reason the Chief won that race.

When they met again, they decided to meet again for another race. They were to be afoot. In the meantime Tseg'sgin' had gone the night before the race and had dug a hole in the road where the race was to be held, had filled it with water, and covered it lightly with brush and dirt.

When morning came, Tseg'sgin' was there first. Then the Chief arrived. He stepped right into the hole and disappeared.

Tseg'sgin' kept calling back, "Why are you afraid of me?"

This was the way Tseg'sgin' won this race.

Yan'sa

Unable to Lose for Winning

The tale entitled "The Indian Munchausen" in SMTS (pp. 262-64) is basically the same as the one we present here in two versions. Swanton collected it among the Natchez Cherokees at some time between 1908 and 1914.

The Natchez Cherokees are a biological and cultural curiosity. Though few and much mixed, they are the descendants of the great Natchez Nation of Mississippi, a people who left no small imprint upon history. Their aboriginal religions and social institutions have provided scholars with many an hour of fascinated bemusement.

After the political destruction of the Natchez in their final war with the French that began on November 28, 1729, some bands of Natchez fled far to the east and ultimately came together as permanent guests of the Cherokees at Gulaniyi, a settlement at the junction of Brasstown Creek with the Hiwassee River near what is now Murphy, North Carolina.[3] Other fugitive Natchez took asylum with the Creeks and amalgamated with them.

The Natchez Cherokees shared with their hosts the inhumanities of the Cherokee Removal of 1838-39 and upon reaching the West settled on both sides of what is now the Sequoyah-Muskogee county line, a few miles south and west of the lower end of Tenkiller Lake. The heart of this district that extends from the environs of the small hill-town of Braggs in Muskogee County to the vicinity of Cedar Springs Baptist Church in Sequoyah County, is

a locale of vague geographical confines known to both Indians and
whites as Nacheetown—spelled, if one has occasion to spell it at
all, in a variety of ways, each signifying "Natcheztown."

Swanton himself was in doubt as to whether any of the stories
he collected among the Natchez Cherokees stemmed from pristine
Natchez sources.[4] Since he found "The Indian Munchausen" only
among the Natchez Cherokees and since we recovered two versions
of it from the Cherokees proper, the inference that the story is of
Cherokee origin is strong. We collected both our versions in the
Nuwôtûn' Ukedaliyû area, in the hills toward the east of Tenkiller
Lake, a few miles, as the crow flies, from the Natchez Cherokee
country.

The Fortunate Hunter

Long ago, a man became ill. When he got well, he was very
hungry.

"I believe that I am able to go to the woods," he thought, so
he got up and went. He took his weapons.

There was a small stream; across it was standing a deer.

"I believe that I can shoot that deer from here," he thought,
and pulled his bow. The arrow went through the deer and struck
a tree near where the deer was standing. [The inference is that the
deer was pinned to the tree.]

He said, "Well, it looks as if I'm going to have to take off my
shoes and get into the water." So he sat down [to remove his
shoes].

Where he sat down, there a rabbit was sitting. As he [the
hunter] busied himself gathering up his belongings he noticed a
rabbit's legs kicking out from beneath him.

Well, he arose, looked down and saw there a rabbit dying from
being sat upon. He picked up the rabbit and struck it against the
ground. Where he struck the ground, a family of quails was sleeping, and they all were killed.

He thought, "I still must take off my shoes." They were high-topped shoes that slipped over his legs [a type of jackboot?]. He took off his shoes and jumped down into the water.

He looked at the deer that was hanging upon the tree. So he went across the stream; but when he got out of the water, he said, "There is something in my shoes⁵ that is pricking me. It must be a lot of small stones."

So he took off his shoes, and when he emptied them out, there was a pile of perch! You see, they [the perch] had gotten into his shoes as he crossed the water, because they piled up as he emptied his shoes. About this size [stretching apart a thumb and a crooked forefinger].

When he put his shoes back on, he pulled the arrow out of the tree and noticed that where the arrow had been, wild honey poured out. [A chuckle.] That tree was the home of bees [i.e., a bee-tree] because honey was pouring out!

He gathered up his fish, took the deer off the arrow, [collected] his rabbit and the quails [and also the honey?]. He shouldered all these things and carried them home.

He was hungry, but life was going to be good now!

That's all.

Gahnô

Tseg'sgin' Goes Hunting

Tseg'sgin', who once lived, went hunting beside a creek. He was hunting deer, and when he had gone quite a way, he saw a deer across the creek. The creek was fairly wide.

Tseg'sgin' had a bow and arrow with him. When he saw the deer, he stopped, aimed at the deer, and shot it. When he discharged his bow, just as the arrow was over the creek, a fish jumped up, and the arrow shot the fish. The arrow went through the deer and stuck into a tree.

Tseg'sgin' wondered how he was going to cross the creek. He had on boots, so he decided to wade the creek. When he got across and went to where the deer was and where the arrow had stuck into the tree, his boots annoyed him. There was something in them. When he took his boots off, they were nearly full of fish.

Then when he got up to get his arrow out of the tree, he had difficulty in getting it out. When he finally did get it out, he pulled so hard that he fell backwards. A family of quails had gone to bed there, and he sat upon them and killed them.

When he got up and looked at the tree again, honey was oozing out. It was a bee-tree. So he hunted for something to plug it with and accidentally grasped a snake. He slammed the snake upon the ground. Then he used his finger to plug up the honey-hole. Finally he remembered he had a handkerchief in his pocket. So he plugged the honey-hole with it, and that made the honey quit wasting away.

                                                            Dalala (M.)

A Tale of a Tail

A Hichiti version of this rollicking story, but with the Rabbit in the role of trickster, appears in SMTS (pp. 114-15), and Swanton notes that Stith Thompson identifies it as a European transplant (also see TMIF, p. 287).

Tseg'sgin' Gets a Woman

Long ago there lived someone called Tseg'sgin'. If he wanted anything, he could always get it. He always found a way to get it.

There was a beautiful woman who lived somewhere that he desired. He didn't know what to do because the woman's father wouldn't let them [Tseg'sgin' and his daughter] go out together. They couldn't be together very much. So Tseg'sgin' had to think quite a long time about it [the existing situation]. He was trying to see how he could manage to marry her.

One time, on his way to see her, he saw cattle in an old field. So he cut off the tail of one of the cows and carried it with him to the woman's house. There were many trees around her home. So just a little way from her home, just out of sight, he stuck the tail into the ground. Then he cried for help so that the father of the woman would hear him.

Sure enough, after a while the father arrived. When he came, Tseg'sgin' said, "My cow went into the ground here. I don't know how I'm going to get her out. If I pull the tail too hard, I might pull it off. Then the cow would disappear forever. Do you have a shovel, or anything that could be used to dig with?" asked Tseg'sgin.'

"I do have," said the man.

"Here! If you'll hold this cow's tail, I'll go get them [digging implements]," said Tseg'sgin'. "Don't you pull it hard. If you do, the cow will be gone forever."

So he went toward the woman's house, and the woman was there alone. She was a young, beautiful woman.

"I saw your father away over there, and he said for us to leave if you want to," he told the young woman.

"I don't believe that my father would say that," she said. "Let me shout to him and ask him," the young woman said.

"All right," said Tseg'sgin'.

So the woman called to her father, "Did you really say so?"

"Yes, that's what I told him!" he said.

So the two of them [Tseg'sgin' and the woman] left. So Tseg'sgin' got his woman because he took her away. That's how Tseg'sgin' found a beautiful woman.

That's all.

Anisgay'dih'

A Modern Myth

Thompson finds the principal motif of this modern myth (probably nineteenth century) among the North American Indians as well as in Indonesia, New Britain, and an assortment of other places (TMIF, p. 369). Here the trickster is ultimately tricked, but one recalls that even the Rabbit was occasionally hoist by his own petard.

The swine was not an American indigene, and one can observe here in midflight the technique of relating some anatomical singularity of an animal to a specific set of circumstances.

Why the Hog's Tail Is Flat

Tseg'sgin'[6] lived somewhere in the forest, and a fierce hog lived nearby. The hog used to kill people. Tseg'sgin' knew a rich [white?] man. He went to the rich man's home and said to the rich man, "I think I can catch that hog that kills people and that everyone fears."

The rich man said, "I don't believe that you can."

Tseg'sgin' said, "I believe that I can. Let's bet." They put up a wager.

So they went together to hunt the hog. Tseg'sgin' took his musical instrument,[7] and when they [Tseg'sgin' and the rich man] got there [where the hog was to be found], Tseg'sgin' got up in a tree and played his musical instrument.

When the hog heard that music, he thought it was very beautiful and drew near. He wanted that musical instrument because he thought the music was so beautiful.

"Well, what can I do to be able to play that way?" he asked.

"I'll teach you," said Tseg'sgin'. "I'll teach you if you'll not kill me when I get down out of this tree."

"I won't kill you," said the hog. "I want to learn to make beautiful sounds."

Well, Tseg'sgin' came down out of the tree and got an ax. He hunted a strong log by chopping about with his ax. Finally he found a log that was very strong. He made a chop with his ax which split the log. Then he called the hog.

"Put your tail in here, and you will hear beautiful music just like you heard a while ago."

The hog thought that that would be true, so he put his tail into the split. Tseg'sgin' removed the ax, and the hog's tail was stuck fast. The hog stood there yelling.

Tseg'sgin' ran to the house of the man with whom he had made
the wager. Tseg'sgin' said to the rich man, "I caught the hog!" So
the [rich] man got his money box and carried it as they [he and
Tseg'sgin'] walked to the place where the hog's tail was fastened.

Well, Tseg'sgin' won the bet, so they counted out the money.
As they were counting out the money, Tseg'sgin' seized the box,
put it upon his shoulder, and ran off with it.

There was a little crack in the box, and as he was running with
the money, the money was leaking out. The rich man followed
and picked up all the money he found along the way.

When Tseg'sgin' stopped and thought he would count his
money, the box was empty—no money! The rich man had picked
up all the coins.

Tseg'sgin' lost, and there was nothing he could do. You see, he
thought he could make more money by taking the box.

Tseg'sgin' was the cause of the hog's tail being flat like it is today because he caught it in the log. (Soft chuckle.)

That's all.

Yan'sa

The Bull Market in Deer

The resale of merchandise previously sold to the dupe is identified in TMIF (p. 263) as an American motif; and indeed, the
backwoods tall-tale flavor of this yarn from the Itsôdiyi community permeates the original Cherokee itself.

Tseg'sgin'[8] Sells His Deer

I'll also tell you another one of the things I heard. I'll tell about
Tseg'sgin' and what he did. He was evil and irresponsible—or
maybe he was clever. We just don't know.

Tseg'sgin' owned a deer. Someone from afar came to Tseg'-
sgin' 's house and wanted the deer. So he [Tseg'sgin'] sold it to
him, and he was well paid for it.

The next morning the man left Tseg'sgin' 's house and led the deer away. Tseg'sgin' ran ahead of the man, and, as soon as he had passed the man, took off one of his shoes, and put it down in the road.

When the man with the deer came to the shoe, he looked at it awhile, and then he went on. Then after awhile he found another shoe where Tseg'sgin' had laid it. The man with the deer arrived there, looked at the shoe, and thought to himself, "This is the same kind of shoe as the other one. This would make a pair. If I had gotten the other one, now I would have had a pair." So he tied his deer by the road and went back for the other shoe.

When he arrived where the first shoe had been, it had disappeared. Tseg'sgin' had already gotten it. So he went back to where he had tied the deer. The shoe that had been there had disappeared, and his deer had disappeared. Tseg'sgin' had gotten the shoe and the deer.

He [the man] ran about hunting his deer. After awhile he thought to himself, "Maybe it ran back home." He returned toward Tseg'sgin' 's house, but Tseg'sgin' had the deer tied in another place. Every time the man walked toward where the deer was tied, Tseg'-sgin' would walk in the opposite direction and make a sound like a deer. Each time he [the man] heard this noise, he would go in that direction. Finally the man had hunted so long that he gave up and went to Tseg'sgin' 's house.

Tseg'sgin' said, "I have another deer. You can have it if you'll pay for it." (But it was the deer that he had previously sold but had recovered and tied up.)

So Tseg'sgin' brought it to him [the man], and the man bought it again. He [Tseg'sgin'] had sold it twice by the time the man took the deer away.

Yan'sa

Tseg'sgin' Eats by Means of Crow

There is a decidedly un-Indian cast to this escapade of Tseg'-sgin', and Thompson does in fact identify its model as being of

European make (TMIF, p. 379). The detail of the pet crow, however, might well be a true Cherokee touch and an old one at that. We read in GTEC (p. 204) that members of the Anitsisqua (Bird) Clan were once given to taming crows and chicken hawks, although we have seen no evidence of this among contemporary Cherokees.

Tseg'sgin' 's Fortunetelling Crow

This Tseg'sgin' we were talking about must have lived a long time ago. At one time he didn't have much money, and he didn't know how to get any money. Then later he thought of this that he could do:

He knew of someone who was courting the wife of somebody else. When the man [husband] went to work, some man came to see his wife; he [the rival] came to her house to see her.

"I'll do something about that!" thought Tseg'sgin'.

He often went in that direction [where she lived]. So he caught himself a crow and tied one of its legs. He carried it around, and he also was watching the house where the man [the husband] lived.

"When the rival comes, I'll go in," he thought.

So when the man [the husband] went to work, the rival came, and Tseg'sgin' went over there [to the house]. He knocked at the door. That scared the visitor so that he had to get under [the house]. Tseg'sgin' then went into the house.

So Tseg'sgin' sat down, and the man [the rival] remained under [the house], and when the man of the house⁹ came, Tseg'sgin' began to pinch the crow's leg, and the crow began to caw. Every once in a while Tseg'sgin' would say to the crow, "You be quiet!" The crow kept on cawing every few minutes. He cawed when he was pinched.

"What's he saying?" asked the man of the house after a while.

"This crow is a fortuneteller. He's telling me that someone is trying to steal your wife. He's really a good fortuneteller. Why don't you buy him from me? I won't charge you too much for him, but he really is a good fortuneteller," he [Tseg'sgin'] said to him [the man of the house]. "Right now he's saying that there's someone under the house."

The visitor under the house heard it [this statement], and he fled. The man of the house believed it [what Tseg'sgin' had told him] about the crow, bought it, and Tseg'sgin' got some money for his fortunetelling crow.

Anisgay'dih'

Tseg'sgin' Gets the First (and Last) Laugh

The familiar "Melancholy Princess" motif is a keystone in each of the three Tseg'sgin' adventures recorded here. The theme of the tables-turning dupe-in-the-bag in the second example is, to be sure, well-nigh world-wide, but although it is known to the American Indians (TMIF, p. 344), the present application of it is certainly European. The "Melancholy Princess" appears as an insert in the longish, un-Cherokeean "literal fool" story told by Siquanid'.

Tseg'sgin' Wins a Wife

Somebody, long ago, had a beautiful woman [daughter] who wouldn't laugh. All the young men desired her.

Tseg'sgin' arrived there, and her father said, "If anyone can make her laugh, I'll give her to him as a wife."

Tseg'sgin' was very clever: he could do anything. So he procured a lean steer with long horns. Then he procured a tow sack and filled it with bones, cans, and just everything. He tied the bag, put it upon the back of the steer, and then mounted the steer.

So he went to the woman's house to make her laugh. He spurred the steer to make him buck, and Tseg'sgin' held on to the steer's tail while he was riding it [backward].

The woman thought that this was funny, so she laughed. So he was given the woman for a wife. She laughed: she thought the bucking steer was funny.

Dôi

Tseg'sgin' Foils His Captors

There was once a king who had a daughter. All of the young men were trying to amuse her because if one of them could make her laugh, he was to have her for a wife.

The men had performed for a long time when Tseg'sgin' came riding up upon a bull. Tseg'sgin' was sitting backward upon the bull. He [the bull] ran in front of the woman, and the bull was bellowing as he ran. The woman laughed.

"Now she laughed at me!" they all said to each other as they squabbled. They were told to keep silent, and the woman was asked at whom she laughed. She said that the man who came by upon the bull made her laugh.

They [the young men] all became angry at the man who had made her laugh, and they said, "Let's take him prisoner!" So they caught him, and they said, "Let's get a sack and throw him into the deep water." They put him into a sack, tied it, and took him down to the water to throw him into it.

While they were getting ready to put him into the water, some-one herding sheep came by. He saw Tseg'sgin' and said, "Why are you in this condition?"

"They're going to take me to the big city where one can choose anything that he wants, but I don't want to go."

The sheepherder said, "I'll go." So the sheepherder untied the bag and let Tseg'sgin' out.

After a while his [Tseg'sgin' 's] captors returned. Tseg'sgin' had already driven the flock of sheep away. When his captors returned, they located the deep water. They took him [the sheepherder that they thought was Tseg'sgin'] to it.

"I'm not the one!"

"Yes, you are! Tseg'sgin', we had you in here!" So they threw him [the sheepherder] into the water.

Later on they saw him [Tseg'sgin'] herding the flock of sheep. "Look at him that we threw into the water!" they said.

"One could choose anything he wanted. He could even get

two women, or the town itself. But I chose herding sheep!" he said.
That's all.

Tlutlu

A *Tseg'sgin'* Saga

We'll tell about the doings of Tseg'sgin' a long time ago:

Once a ferryman hired a man to work for him taking people across a large river. He [the hired man] lived near the river, and Tseg'sgin' came around [visited] often. He [?] was walking all around the flatboat, and people who were traveling were arriving at the water's edge.

The river must have been very large, according to the way I heard it [the story]. When travelers arrived, the hired hand ferried them across. When he got them across, they paid him something— they gave him a chicken or a hog or a cow. The hired hand was having great difficulty in ferrying people (even the owner had to work): too many people wanted to go across.

Tseg'sgin' was around often, visiting. "I'm going to [approach] Tseg'sgin' when he comes," he [the owner] thought. "I'm going to tell him to ferry these people across for me on the flatboat." (Tseg'-sgin' was living with his grandmother in those days.)

Afterwhile Tseg'sgin' appeared and came to the ferryman's house. The ferryman was very glad to see him. "I'm very glad that you came," he said. "Where I take people across, you're going to do it for me. I'm going to hire you. And when they [the customers] pay you, you just accept whatever they give you for taking them across. It will be yours, whatever you get."

"All right," said Tseg'sgin'.

Tseg'sgin' was standing there by the water, waiting to take people across. Afterwhile a wagonload of travelers came. When they got on the boat and he took them across, he took the wagon, the horses, and everything that they had. When they got across, they paid him. (In those days they paid with animals, or anything that they might possess—even pins or butter. Even cattle—those who owned them.)

The first people he ferried across paid him with a needle. He put his needle upon a log while he helped the travelers repack. When the travelers had moved on, he thought to himself, "I'll go get my needle now." But he couldn't find it. He hunted the needle all around on the ground and on the log and couldn't find it anywhere. Then he went home to his grandmother.

When he arrived at his grandmother's house that evening, "Grandmother," Tseg'sgin' said.

"What is it?" said the old woman.

"Some while ago I ferried some people across and they gave me a needle for my pay. I put it upon a log. Later when I decided to get it, I couldn't find it," said Tseg'sgin'.

"You're very foolish," said his grandmother to Tseg'sgin'. "People pin something like that to their clothes."

"All right. Next time I'll pin it on me," said Tseg'sgin'.

When he arrived at the river very early the next morning, travelers were already there. He took them across, and they gave him a good-sized pig for his pay. When the travelers had gone on, he began to wonder what to do with his pig. "My grandmother told me, 'People pin something like that to their clothes,'" he thought. He picked up the pig and attempted to pin it to his clothes. The pig kicked so much that it tore his clothes, and he couldn't pin it. So he chased after the travelers and returned the pig to them. He told them he couldn't pin the pig to his clothes.

When he got home that evening, he said, "Grandmother, today I was given a pig for my pay, but I couldn't pin it to my clothes, and it tore my clothes all up."

"You are the most foolish man! People hobble the feet of things like that and lead them home," she said.

"All right. Next time I'll do that," he said.

So the next morning he went very early, and there people were already waiting to be taken across. So he took them across. When he got them across, he helped them to reload their wagon, and so they started off. They had paid him with a large rooster; so he tied the legs of the rooster, and the rooster flopped and flopped and flopped. It was unable to walk. So he kept kicking at it, trying to lead it, but it wouldn't be led. When he gave up trying to lead it, he untied the rooster's legs and chased after the people he had taken across. When they had gone about a mile, he finally caught up with them.

"I brought the chicken back. I tied its legs, but it couldn't walk with its feet tied," he told them. When he gave it to them, they were happy to get it back.

So Tseg'sgin' went home. When he arrived home, he said, "Grandmother, you told me that when people were presented things with legs, you tied their legs. They gave me a large chicken, a rooster, and I tied its legs, but it wouldn't go. It just flopped about," he said.

"I'm really getting tired of your foolishness, man!" he was told. "You just can't learn anything!" he was told.

"All right. Next time then," he said.

So the very next morning when he arrived near the river, people were already there, waiting to be taken across. They had two wagonloads to be taken across. So these two [owners of the wagons] agreed to share the payment.

(When I was talking about that chicken, I forgot something. He [Tseg'sgin'] had been told that when people were given something with legs, like chickens, they tie their legs and shoulder them. So he had said when he had been told that, "All right. Next time I'll do that.")

They had two wagons there ready for him to take across. So the owners of the two wagons agreed to share the payment. "We'll just give him a horse, and that will pay for both of us," they said.

So he took them across, and they paid him with a beautiful horse, a black and handsome one. When they left, he had it tied nearby. So he began to tie the horse's legs. He tried all day to shoulder it. It was too heavy. He kept swaying back and forth. So he finally gave up trying to shoulder the horse with the tied legs.

He went after the people who had given him the horse and finally caught up with them far down the way and gave them back the horse.

When he returned to his grandmother: "This time I was given a huge, beautiful horse, and I tied his legs, but I just couldn't shoulder him," said Tseg'sgin'.

"You are really foolish, aren't you?" he was told. "People ride horses. Anything with four legs they ride."

"All right. Next time then," he said.

So when he arrived at the river the next morning there were people already waiting to be taken across. So he took them across. When they got across and got everything loaded up, they gave him a cow for his pay and left. He stood there thinking about what to do.

On that same day, in the same direction that the travelers were going, there was a large city. There was a wealthy king who lived there, and he had a beautiful daughter who had never laughed. All of the young men were going to gather there and do all sorts of tricks in order to make her laugh.

All the young men were performing the best they could. She was placed up high upon a balcony where she could look down and see them. They had two men to watch her to see if she laughed. The wealthy king sat nearby.

Tseg'sgin' was given a cow—(this woman had never laughed; she always had an angry look)—at that time when Tseg'sgin' was given a cow, he stood there a long while thinking about what to do. He thought, "Now what can I do with her? I can't put a bit on her. Look at how she looks! She's a cow!" So he finally decided to ride the cow backward and hold her tail (he could stay upon her by holding her tail); so he got upon her backward, held the cow by her tail, and rode away as fast as he could.

The cow went in the direction of the city, and when she went toward the big town, there was a large crowd there, and all the young men were doing their tricks. But the King's daughter did not laugh—and there were two men who watched her to see if she did laugh.

The King's daughter was looking out toward the road, and she saw the man upon the cow running into town. She thought, "I wonder why that man is riding backward." When she took a good look, she saw that the man was riding by holding the tail. He was riding backward.

So the King's daughter opened her mouth and laughed, and when all the young men noticed that she was laughing, they all said, "She's laughing at me! She's laughing at me!" said the young men. "No! It is me that she is laughing at!" they all said, and they began fighting right in the middle of the street. They were fighting over the young woman. So this fight continued until it looked like a battle.

The King stepped down and said, "Get quiet awhile! Let's just ask the young woman at whom she laughed—and let's ask her if she really laughed," he said as he stepped down to the ground.

So they asked the two men who had been watching her. When they asked them, they [the two men] said, "It was the man who rode backward on a cow, holding the tail, that she laughed at. She was looking at him when she laughed."

"That's who can have her," said the King. "Where did that man go?"

They finally caught up with Tseg'sgin'. "You just won a beautiful woman when you rode by through town," they told him, "and half of the kingdom will be given to you by the King." So Tseg'sgin' was given the beautiful woman, a rich woman. Then he let the cow go—he preferred the woman!

The King told Tseg'sgin', "You have to take her for your wife and go somewhere and make a home."

"All right. We'll go." So they left immediately. They traveled on foot.

Afterwhile it began to get dark, but there were no houses about. They came to the edge of a forest and saw nothing but prairie.

There was not a house anywhere. After they had walked about half of the length of the prairie, they saw the tip of a house. They saw smoke coming out of the chimney.

Tseg'sgin' said, "Somebody lives there. Let's stay all night there."

She [his wife] said, "All right. Let's stay there, regardless of who lives there."

"All right."

So they walked toward it [the house], and they arrived there. It was now nearly sundown. When they arrived there, Tseg'sgin' looked into the house. Only a very old woman, sitting there sewing, was inside; but there was also a child, about three years old, crawling about on the floor near the old woman.

When the old woman saw Tseg'sgin', she said, "What do you want?"

"Night has come upon us. Could we stay all night with you? We want to stay just this one night. We still have far to go," said Tseg'sgin'.

"All right. You can stay all night here. The only thing [difficulty] is, I don't have anything to cook for your supper. I have to go too far to get my wood. You see, there aren't any trees here on the prairie. I always have to go so far to gather my wood. I have to go where those trees are that you can see from here," said the old woman.

Tseg'sgin' said, "Well, we'll take care of the baby for you."

"All right. I'd be happy if you'd do that, and I'll go for the wood right now, and then we'll eat supper together tonight," said the old woman.

So Tseg'sgin' told his wife, "Now let's take care of the baby."

"All right," she said. Then Tseg'sgin''s beautiful wife said, "If there is a little wood around here, I could start the supper."

Tseg'sgin' was playing with the baby as it was crawling about. As the old woman was leaving, she said to the young woman, "That baby gets soiled sometimes. When he does, and you change him, put the clothes in the barrel that is sitting outside, and when you think that they are soaked enough, put them on top of the house," the old woman told the young woman, Tseg'sgin' 's wife.

"All right," she said.

Away afterwhile the baby needed cleaning. He soiled his diaper. Tseg'sgin' noticed it. "Hey!" he said to his wife. "Hey! The baby has soiled himself. What did the old woman say when she left?" said Tseg'sgin'.

"She said that whenever the baby became soiled, to change him and put the clothes in a barrel," she said.

"All right."

Tseg'sgin' took the baby and the clothes and put them both in the barrel. It smothered in its dirty clothes in the barrel. Just about the time the old woman was coming home, Tseg'sgin' took the clothes and the baby and put them on top of the house.

When the old woman came home, she said, "Where's the baby?"

"I'm drying him on top of the house," said Tseg'sgin'.

"You've killed my baby!" the old woman said. "I think you're very wicked people, and I want you to leave right now!" So they were told to leave the house before they had their supper.

So they left, and it was dark as they were walking. Finally they came to an old deserted house. It had a beautiful white door. Tseg'-sgin' saw the door, and he said, "Let's stay all night here, and we can continue our trip tomorrow," said Tseg'sgin'.

She said, "All right."

They spent the night in this deserted house. They didn't have anything to eat, and they were starving.

The next morning they got ready to leave. Tseg'sgin' said, "Isn't this a beautiful door? I'm going to take it off and carry it with me."

"No! Leave it alone!" she said. "You can't carry a big thing like that. You'll get tired."

"No, I'm going to take it," he said as he took it off its hinges.

So he shouldered it as they walked up the road. After they had traveled awhile, they heard a noise. It sounded like people talk-ing. They kept hearing the noise, and they finally decided that it came from behind a hill. Then they saw a clearing in which there was a huge crowd of people having a meeting. The gathering was composed of all sorts of people, and they were collecting money for the community.

Tseg'sgin' said, "What are we going to do?"

There was a huge tree nearby that leaned over and shaded the spot where they were collecting the money. So they climbed the tree that was leaning over. As they were climbing, he was carrying the door upon his back, and she was following him.

She said to him, "Don't drop that! They'll see us climbing this tree."

"They won't see us," he said.

They were directly over the table upon which the money was being collected. The people didn't see them. They [the people] had collected so much money that the table was loaded.

"I'm certainly tired of carrying this door upon my back! I'm going to drop it," said Tseg'sgin'.

"No! Don't you do it! They'll see us if you drop it," said his wife.

"But I'm tired!" said Tseg'sgin'.

After a while he lost his grip upon it, and it went "Quô! Quô! Quô! Quô! Quô!!" as it went down, snapping off limbs. The horses [of the people assembled] were frightened. They broke their tethers and ran away, and all the people fled. All the people disappeared, but they left the table piled high with money.

So they [Tseg'sgin' and his wife] came down out of the tree. He said, "Let's get the money!" So Tseg'sgin' filled a tow sack full of money. Now they were rich.

That's as far as I know. That's the end of it.

Siquanid'

TALES OF HUMOR

DƏWY ᎪᏋᎾᎳR ᏅᎥᎠᏲ ᏊᏘᎯᎯ
ᎪᏍᏗ ᎾᏍᏃ ᎣᏣᏣ ᏦᎳᏫᎬᏍ

"The Cherokee said, 'It will rain today because I heard a hoot owl.'"

TALES OF HUMOR

"WHERE THERE IS A WILL . . ."

The Cherokees possess a delicious sense of humor, most of which is hidden from outsiders behind a language barrier. But upon the basis of these few samples that we offer here, one might conceivably receive a distorted picture; for the crowning glory of Cherokee wit is a scintillating satire couched in dry understatement. And this is not represented here.

In one sense, it is to be regretted that no one has yet skimmed the cream of Cherokee jest and brought it to public attention; but in another sense, the whole world had it in the most characteristic form, and for many years, in Will Rogers, the greatest humorist the Cherokee people ever produced.

The reason that the Cherokees venerate the genial shade of Rogers is not because he brought them fame. No people can do as nicely without fame as they. It is because he was the archetype of the uncounted and unsung many of his tribesmen who skilfully practice the healing art of cheerfulness.

Worm-Eaters in the Garden

The oversensitive, mentally underequipped individual in contemporary American society is rarely considered material for comedy, but to the Cherokees he is fair game. To these people, proverbially grave, but serene and cheerful, the pouter stands out in the crowd and earns for himself a small but secure place in oral tradition.

The Sensitive Suitor

A man went to a woman's house. This woman was a widow, and this man was her suitor. He sat upon her kanon'.[1] The man wanted to live there with her,[2] so he said to her, "If you don't mind, I'd like to sit here always." (He was sitting upon her kanon'.)

"I suppose that wouldn't do because I have to use that kanon' every day to make my kanohen',"[3] she told him.

The man became piqued and left.

Dôi

The Disgruntled Diner

It is said that someone was invited to eat somewhere. At noon he was told, "Let's go eat some bread." So when they [the diners] went into the dining room, they all sat down. Immediately he picked up his bread. That's all he ate.

"Maybe you would like this"—as they offered him food.

He would say, "No, this is enough."

"Maybe this?" they asked him of other foods.

"No, this is enough," he kept replying.

"Maybe you want something else that is upon the table. If so, ask for it."

"No. I don't want any."

Then they asked him, "Aren't you hungry?"

"Well, you said for us to go eat bread," he told them.

"I was just joking when I said that," he was told. The man was piqued.

Diyôhli

The Weather Doesn't Agree with the Owl

This little joke is a fairly representative sampling of a simple and barbless strain of humor that flows through our Nature-loving and Nature-knowing people.

The Inexperienced Owl[4]

Someone said that once a white man said to a Cherokee (it had not rained for a long, long time), "It is so dry—it has not rained in so long! When do you think it will rain?"

The Cherokee said, "It will rain today because I heard a hoot owl."

The white man said, "You are very wise."

But some days later the white man met the Cherokee and asked him why it had not rained when he said that it would rain.

"Well, the hoot owl said it was going to rain, and when he says it is going to rain, it usually does. But this one happened to be a very young one who didn't know anything yet."

That's all I know.

Ganahw'sôsg'

The Poor Man's Paganini and the Poltergeists

The motif of the man gulled into spending the night in a haunted house girdles the globe. Yan'sa's tale offers us a slight difference: the dupe is cajoled into making his stay atop a poltergeist-infested house.

The Cherokees, incidentally, must surely be among the most musically gifted of all Indians, and since initial contact with Europeans have prized and cultivated square dance fiddle-playing.

The Unsuccessful Fiddler

These are the happenings of long ago that I have heard about:

There was a man who wanted to learn to play the fiddle. He couldn't learn. Sometimes he wondered what he could possibly do to learn to play.

Later on a man wanted to play a trick on him; so he said to him, "If you will find a very old house, get up on the roof, sit upon an eave, and dangle your legs down, and play upon your fiddle, you'll learn to play," he was told.

The man was just teasing him; but because he so much wanted to play, he decided to do just as the man had told him to do and got on top of the house. (This house was abandoned.)

When he started [to play], he heard a noise beneath him. Then he heard dancing beneath him. Then someone took the fiddle away

from him. Then he heard music playing, but he couldn't see anyone [playing it]. (And the fiddle had been taken away from him!)
Then the fiddle was handed back to him. He was being teased more
and more.

After a while the dancing was much nearer, but the man went
on playing his music. He was becoming better and better. Later he
was kicked by someone, but he kept on playing his music. Then
later on he was slapped, but the man continued playing.

Then a bright light was shined in his face. It became bright
all around him. Then he became exceedingly frightened; so he
jumped down to the ground, fell upon his fiddle, and smashed it.
And he forgot all the music he had learned.

He [really] didn't learn anything. He hurt himself for nothing.
(Laugh.)

Yan'sa

MISCELLANEOUS STORIES

ᏓᎤᏃ ᎠᏥᏍᎤᏌᎥᎠᏘ ᎦᎷᏆᏃ ᏆᏓᎥ
ᏔᏣᏔᏍᎤᏃ

"They say corn had its beginning from a human being . . ."

MISCELLANEOUS STORIES

NOT FITTING, BUT PROPER

While the term "miscellaneous" bears some slight popular connotation of inferiority, we do not feel that this, our catchall category, consists of editorial dregs. "The Origin of Corn," for example, is a magnificent myth, and the two Thunder stories enjoy at least one claim to importance—that of appearing in their original presentation. The stories proffered here merely do not fit into any of the other, quite arbitrary, classifications.

A New Version of a Classic

"The Origin of Corn" is, to be sure, one of the best known of all Indian cosmogonic myths, Cherokee or otherwise. It is represented in MMOC (pp. 242-49) and in MMOC (1888) (pp. 97 ff.) by fairly extensive treatment and echoed in SMTS by Creek, Natchez Cherokee, and Koasati contributions.

The version that we came upon differs significantly in detail from them all; but its most cherishable difference lies in its emotional qualities. Or so it seems. This may be due to the respective techniques employed in transcription. All the others appear to be essentially retellings of the myth in English; we translated directly from the verbal text.

The Origin of Corn

I think that these stories [the ones he had been telling] are very interesting. From my childhood they have been interesting to me.

At one time there was a very old woman who had two grandsons. These two grandsons were always hunting. They hunted deer and wild turkeys. They [the family] always had plenty to eat.

Later on, after many hunting trips, when they got ready to go hunting early in the morning, they were cleaning their guns. When their grandmother noticed that they were ready to go [hunting], she thought to herself, "They are getting ready to go hunting"; so she went to them where they were cleaning their guns, outside the fenced-in yard.

When the grandmother came to them, they were busily cleaning their guns. She said to them, "I see that you are getting ready to go hunting," and they replied, "Yes. We are going to hunt deer today."

"Well, when you come back, I'll have the most delicious of dinners ready. I'm going to cook all of the old meat [meat on hand], and I'm going to put into it something they call corn,[1] and we're going to drink the broth from it," she said to the young men.

"All right," said the young men.

When they got to the forest, they wondered about the word "corn" that she had used. They didn't know what that was, and they wondered where she got it.

"I wonder where corn comes from?" they asked each other. "When we get home, we'll find out," they said. They killed a deer, shouldered it, and went home.

When they got home, they saw the large pot bubbling. They noticed that with the meat corn in small ground-up pieces was boiling in there. (If anyone had ever seen it before, he would have known what it was; but then these boys had never seen it before.)

They asked their grandmother, "What is that that you have in the pot?"

"It is called grits."[2]

They didn't ask her where she got it.

When they ate their dinner, the young man had the most delicious meal that they had ever had. After dinner they told their grandmother what a superb meal she had cooked. The grandmother was pleased.

"Well, tomorrow at noon³ we will have some more delicious food."

The next day they [the young men] went hunting again, but they [the family] already had [on hand] some dried [smoked?] turkeys. So the grandmother cooked these dried turkeys and cooked grits with them.

When they [the young men] returned home that evening with their bag of turkeys, dinner was announced. With this meat were these grits, and the young men said, "This is the best meal that we have ever had." They thanked their grandmother again and told her that her food was delicious.

The grandmother was very pleased and said, "I'm so happy that you said what you did."

Next day they [the young men] again went to the forest. While they were in the forest, one of them kept thinking about the corn. "This thing she calls corn . . . She said that today about noon she is going to start cooking again," said one to the other; and the other said, "Yes, that's what she said."

"I'll go hide around somewhere and see where she gets it if you want me to," said one.

"All right," said the other. "You had better go before she begins cooking."

So one of them went. This thing called corn was troubling this young man; so he hid behind the smokehouse and watched for his grandmother.

Later on the grandmother came carrying a large pan and went into the smokehouse. The young man peeped through a small hole. When the grandmother got into the smokehouse, she put the pan under where she was standing. Then she struck both of her sides, and when she hit her sides grits fell from every part of her body. They fell until the pan became full. When she came out of the smokehouse, she carried this pan of grits, dumped them into the pot, and began cooking them.

That's what the young man learned, and he went back to his

brother and told him about it. When he arrived where his brother was, his brother asked him what he had learned.

He said to his brother, "This delicious food of grandmother's that we have been eating comes from her body. She shakes it off from all over her body. She puts a pan under her. She strikes her sides, and it falls off her body and falls into the pan until it is full, and that is what we have been eating," he told his brother.

His brother said, "We really eat an unsavory thing, don't we!" So they decided that they would not eat any more of it when they got home.

When they arrived home, their grandmother had dinner ready. Again she had the same kind of food. They both didn't eat much.

"What's wrong? You're not eating very much. Don't you like me?" said their grandmother.

The young men said, "No.⁴ We're just too tired [to eat much] from walking so much in our hunting."

"But I think that you don't like me," she said. "Or maybe you learned something somewhere, and that's the reason that you don't want to eat," they were told.

At that moment the grandmother became ill. She knew that they had found out [her secret]. The grandmother took to bed, and she began to talk to them about what they should do.

"Now that I'm in bed, I'm going to die." (She told them all about what was going to happen in the future.) "When you bury me, you must put a large fence around me and bury me just right out there. Something will grow from right in the middle of my grave. This thing will grow up to be tall. It will flower at the top, and in the lower part will come out beautiful tassels, and inside of them will be kernels. It will bear two or three ears of corn with cornsilk on them.

"You must leave the ears alone and take care of the plant. Put a fence around it. They [the ears] will dry; they will be very white; the shuck will be brown and crisp; and the silk will be dark brown. That is when you gather it.

"This thing they call corn is I. This corn will have its origin in me.

"You must take the kernels off the cob and plant them. Store them away until spring. When spring comes, make spaced-out holes in the ground and put about two of the kernels in each hole. By doing this you will increase your supply—and it is surpassingly good food—and when it sprouts, it will go through the various stages of growth that you will have seen in this one [plant] of mine.

"Then it will bear corn that you can use, either to boil (boiled corn is very good to eat all summer long, while it is green) or in winter you can use it to make meal.

"I will be the Corn-Mother," said the old woman (a long time ago, they said).

That's the injunction that the young men were taught to carry out. They thought about this deeply as they were burying her after she died. After they buried her, they made the fence; and all that summer it [the corn plant] grew and bore corn just as she told them it would do, and when the corn became dry, they gathered it and took the kernels off the cobs.

Then again next spring they planted it. Then the two young men said, "It would be better if we each had a wife."

One of the young men said, "Let's just one of us get a wife. You get a wife, and I'll be a bachelor and live with you."

The other said, "All right," and left to search for a wife.

The young man said to the one who left to get a wife, "Just walk some distance over there, blow your [cupped?] hands [making a whistling noise], and there will be a girl run to you."

So he [the young man searching for a wife] arrived [at a destination] away off into the forest near a house, I believe. In that house was an old couple with a large number of young women [daughters]. These young women were all outside playing. Some of these young women were frolicking about, and others were laughing and making a lot of noise.

The young man came quite near, blew into his hands, and whistled. One of the young women who was playing stopped and said, "I'm going to stop playing because someone is whistling for me," and left the group.

She ran directly to the young man. The young man said to her, "We'll marry, if it's all right with you."

She said, "All right." So they went to his home.

The young man told her that in the spring they would plant corn, and each year they would plant more and more of it. So when spring came, they used their hoes to make holes so that they could plant corn. They hoed and hoed and had a very large field of corn, and that was the beginning of there being so much corn. And they [the young men] remembered what the old woman had said to them, "I will be the Corn-Mother," she had said. "Don't ever forget where I am buried," she had told them when she talked to them.

From this beginning there became so much corn that everyone in the whole world had some. They say that corn had its beginning from a human being, that the plant called corn started from a woman, and that when this [young] man took a wife, they had such a huge field that they had much corn and much food to eat.

That's what I know, and that's the end of it: that's all.

Siquanid'

Fish Story

Tlutlu's little story below is another example of the tall tale, and is cognate with "The Fortune Hunter."

The Fisherman and the Gobbler

There was a fisherman sitting upon the bank. For a long time nothing tugged at his line. Finally, something took his line, and when he jerked it (he was sitting upon a lower bank), the fish flew over his head and landed on the hillside behind him. He began pulling his line back, and when he pulled it, a gobbler landed!

So he got the gobbler—and they say that he got both the fish and the gobbler.

That's all. *That's all.*

Tlutlu

Junior Partner

Dalala (M.) pretends to no professionalism in storytelling, yet in a session with him very late one night he recalled and related a myth that was completely new to us: we had never heard it before nor had we seen it in print.

Thunder and the Turtle

One time Thunder and the Turtle were talking. The Turtle asked Thunder to be his fighting partner. So Thunder asked the Turtle, "What can you do?"

He [the Turtle] immediately ran and jumped over a small stick and broke off a small piece of it.[5]

"This is what I can do," he said as he returned. "What can you do?" he asked Thunder.

Thunder said, "I can do this." He created lightning. It struck a tree and tore it into splinters.

The Turtle ran away and went into the water, and that's when his living in the water began. He was afraid of Thunder, and that's why he lives in the water today.

Because he became frightened by Thunder at that time, today when it rains and thunders, he doesn't come out of the water. He thought that Thunder was fierce when he shredded the tree. It frightened him forever. So they never became fighting partners.

Dalala (M.)

Senior Partner

We raise the question as to whether the primary role assigned to Thunder in Cherokee theology by the Oklahoma contemporary conservatives and the secondary role discovered for this deity in

North Carolina by Mooney and Olbrechts in their era is due to different cultural time levels, spatial factors, insufficient investigation, lack of linguistic facility, or some other cause or causes. At any rate, this discrepancy is a fact that future scholarship must face. Certainly this myth, apparently printed here for the first time, subsumes for Thunder an unequivocal position.

Thunder Deputizes the Eagle

We'll talk about Thunder-Lightning[6] and the Eagle. They say that Thunder and the Eagle are fast friends.

Long ago, Thunder spoke to every wild creature—everything that flew or everything with four legs—and to the Eagle he said, "I appoint you Ruler.[7] You must have a meeting with all wild creatures, and you must answer all their requests. If you think they [the creatures] should be a certain way, you make them that way. You must ask them what they want to be," said Thunder.

So the Eagle called a meeting. All kinds of birds[8] came to it. When they arrived, the meeting was called to order. He [the Eagle] asked each of them what he wanted to be able to do.

The Quail, who was very selfish when asked about anything, immediately arose and went and stood beside the Eagle.

"Couldn't you give me power so that when a man sees me fly, he will instantly die of fright?" the Quail asked the Eagle.

"No," said the Eagle. "You are entirely too small. I could not give you that kind of power. But I can go this far: I can let you fly, and when a man hears you fly, he will become frightened," said the Eagle to the Quail.

The Quail said, "All right."

That's the reason why when we hear one [a quail] flying, we become frightened because he makes a whirring noise. That's all the power he was allowed.

Next came the Terrapin that crawls on land. "I would like to be able to produce a poison that kills people. Allow me that kind of power," he said to the Eagle.

"No," said the Eagle. "You are entirely too slow and too small."

Thunder and the Eagle had a conference. (Thunder was the Ruler of all the Earth and Heaven.[9] That's why he appointed his best friend as Ruler of the Earth.)

The thing I [especially?] remember about the doings of the Eagle is that he gave a power to the Chickadee. He [the Chickadee] was given the power to be something like a fortuneteller among people in that he could go where people were, and if they were going to have visitors, he could inform them ahead of time. This could be done by flying to a tree near them and singing a joyous song.[10]

"Would you give me that kind of power?" asked the Chickadee. So he was given that power. That's why the Cherokees say when they see a chickadee fly into a tree, "The Chickadee says somebody is coming." That's the power that was given to him, they say.

Then the Redbird, the beautifully singing bird, came up: "Let people have faith in me. I want to be able to sing joyful songs when it is going to rain."

So he was given that power. That's why the old Cherokees all believe that when they see this bird singing atop a tree, it will rain. That's all the power he was given.

The Shrike[11] came up and said, "All I want is to be an expert dance-caller." And so he was given that power.

Said the people long ago: the Eagle was the Ruler of the Earth, but Thunder was the Ruler of the whole Universe, and they got together to decide if all of their distributed powers were going to be satisfactory. So said the people of long ago.

That's all I know.

Siquanid'

ETHNOLOGICAL DATA

ᏃᏍᏗ ᎠᏍ ᎠᏫ ᎠᏂᎵ

"A big fire in the center . . ."

ETHNOLOGICAL DATA

Q.E.D.

Our tapes were found to contain many sidelights on the primitive religion, choreography, social structure, amusements, and patterns of thought of the Cherokees, past and present. By the excision and presentation here of some of the representative passages we are aware, of course, of having provided more questions than answers. We merely point up the existing need for scholarly investigation into every aspect of Cherokee culture while the opportunity for its application is still present.

Little Deer

Those spirit animals, Ahw'usti (Little Deer) and Ahw'equ' (Big Deer), are ubiquitous in the oral folklore and in the literature on Cherokee folk belief (for example, see MMOC, pp. 250-51, 262-64). The literature, by the way, but barely hints at the importance attached to these beings and does not mention at all certain roles that they play in the Indian's thought-world—notably the tutelary one touched upon by Dôi in his confirmation of Ahw'usti's being a lar who lived in the house.

We proffer two accounts of personal experience with Ahw'usti.

Dôi on Ahw'usti

ANNA G. KILPATRICK: Did you ever hear of Ahw'usti?

DOI: I have, but I have forgotten [what I heard].

A.G.K.: I wonder what he was like. They ["the old people"] claim that they fed him.[1]

D.: Yes, they did [feed him].

A.G.K.: Was he like a man, like a dog, or like a deer?

D.: He was a deer, very small deer.

A.G.K.: He lived in the house, didn't he?

D.: Yes. He was a small creature [indicating a foot and one-half or so].

A.G.K. (observing the measurement): He was small, a small creature, wasn't he? They used to tell about them [spirit animals] a long time ago, didn't they?

D.: Yes, they did, didn't they?

A.G.K.: Did you ever see any of these creatures?

D.: I have seen a head of Ahw'usti. It had horns. His head was a very small object [indicating], and his horns were very tiny. *Had horns on, like . . . like goat.* Very much like one.

A.G.K.: When did you see it?

D.: Someone had it. I just saw it, that's all.

A.G.K.: Did you see the skull, the *bone?*

D.: Yes, that's it—just the bone. Ahw'equ' and Ahw'usti both lived.

A.G.K.: What did they call Ahw'equ'?

D.: Just Ahw'equ'. That's all I know. Ahw'equ' had big horns.

A.G.K.: Was he large?

D.: Large.

A.G.K.: What do you call him in English? *Elk?*

D.: Yes, that's it—*Elk.* That's what they call that creek down there—Elk Creek.[2] *Elk.* That's it.

A.G.K.: Elk Creek?

D.: They call it Elk Creek. That's the name—Elk Creek.

A.G.K.: Did they have elk in this area a long time ago?

D.: Yes, a long time ago they did—long time ago.

A.G.K.: What did they use them for?

D.: I don't know. But there were bears here, too.

A.G.K.: Yes, they lived here, didn't they?

D.: There were lions[3] . . .

A.G.K.: There were lions?

D.: Yes. There were some lions that were long and striped, and then there were very small-sized ones. There was a striped kind, and the small ones were like dogs.

A.G.K.: And this Ahw'usti—did you say that they "used" him for "medicine"?

D.: I don't know. The old people who lived long ago used to "use" him. And they loved him.

A.G.K.: That's true.

D.: And they were fond of Ahw'equ', too.

A.G.K.: They "used" both of them for "medicine"?

D.: Yes, both. They knew a lot, these people who lived long ago.

Asudi on Ahw'usti

ANNA G. KILPATRICK: What about Ahw'usti that they tell about?

ASUDI: He's still living. Up there on the hill, straight through here [indicating], there is a salt spring. In Asûwôsg' Precinct,[4] a long time ago, I was walking by there, hunting horses. There was a little trail that went down the hill (nowdays there is a big highway on that hill up there), and farther up on the flat the road divided. Beyond that, in the valley near Ayôhli Amayi,[5] hunting horses early in the morning, I was walking there in the valley when I saw them[6] walking, and I stopped in amazement.

They were this [indicating a foot] high and had horns. The first one was just this [indicating as before] high, and he had horns. They were beautiful, and they were going in that [indicating] direction. There were no houses there. It was in the forest, and I wondered where they were going. Several in number, they were all walking. He [Ahw'usti] was going first, just this [indicating] high, and he had horns. His horns were just as my hands are shaped —five. *Five points,* they call them five points. That's the way it was. Just this [indicating] high, and so beautiful! And there was a second one, third one, fourth one. The fifth one was a huge one, and he also had horns with five points.

They stopped awhile, and they watched me. I was so afraid of the large ones! They were turning back, looking at me. They were pawing with their feet, and I was truly afraid then! They were showing their anger then. First they would go [paw with the] right [hoof] and then [with the] left and go: "Ti! Ti! Ti! Ti!" They kept looking at me and pawing, and I just stood still.

They started again and disappeared away off, and I wondered where they went. I heard my horses over there [?], and I went there as quickly as I could. I caught me a horse [to ride?] and took the others home.

There was a man named Tseg' Ahl'tadeg',[7] and when I arrived there [at his home?], he asked me, "What was it that you learned today?"

"I saw an amazing thing down there," I told him.

"What was it?"

"A deer. He was just this [indicating] high, and he had horns like this [indicating], and he was walking in front. The second one was this [indicating] high, and the third one was this [indicating] high, and [also] the fourth one—then the rest were large."

"It was Ahw'usti," he said.

Asudi

Not a Sorcerer's Best Friend

Cherokee demonology is a whole world of thought, attitudes, and emotions within itself, and so encapsulated is it, that the sociological studies of it that we have seen, scholarly as they are, strike us as being based upon views from too far outside. It is a vaster world than one might suspect, and far more complex.

The occult is a subject that your average Cherokee conversationally touches upon reluctantly and furtively. This makes all the more remarkable the following conversation in which an aged brother and sister accuse each other of witchcraft! We had never expected to hear such a verbal passage of arms, let alone to get one down on tape.

Gahnô and Dalala (N.) Accuse Each Other of Witchcraft

GAHNO: That dog hates Dalala,[8] nobody else.[9]

ANNA G. KILPATRICK: Dalala, Dalala! Why doesn't this dog like you?

DALALA: Huh?

A.G.K.: Why doesn't he like you?

D.: I don't know. He just doesn't have much sense.

G.: He [Dalala] gets angry at him [the dog], and the dog doesn't like him. The dog hates him all the time. He would grab at Dalala if I didn't shout at the dog all the time. He [Dalala] always carries a long stick. He [the dog] really dislikes him because he [Dalala] is a sorcerer. Dogs don't like that kind of person. Sorcerers are night-travelers,[10] and that is the reason that the dog doesn't like him.

A.G.K. (to Dalala): Is this true?

D.: Huh?

A.G.K.: Is it true?

D.: She's a witch herself. I've seen her.[11]

A.G.K.: When?

D.: Huh?

A.G.K.: When?

D.: About six or seven years ago.

A.G.K.: Speak into this [the microphone].

D.: That?

A.G.K. (to Jack F. Kilpatrick, who was adjusting the tape recorder): *When you get through there, let him tell you how he saw her as a witch.*

D.: I saw her about six or seven years ago. I was in the hospital. She came there. She's a witch. I was in the hospital six or seven years ago—maybe longer ago than that. As I was lying there, I saw her, this old woman (she's my sister, you know). There was a place up high [a window high in the wall?] where one could see out, and that's where she appeared. I saw her just down to the arms. Her arms were short and had feathers on them. She was

doing like this [demonstrating], shaking her arms, and her feathers
were going, "Shi! Shi! Shi! Shi! Shi!" and she was looking at me.
I kept looking at her, and she kept coming toward me, and she
looked [in the face?] exactly like she looks today. It was she, and
she was coming nearer, and I kept looking at her. I wasn't dream-
ing. I was seeing her. She kept coming toward me, and I kept
watching her until she got very close, and I said, "Heh!" and did
this [warding-off motion]. That's all I saw. I know she's a witch.

G. (who is quite deaf): What did you tell?

A.G.K.: Did you ever see him as a sorcerer?

G.: Let's see . . . well . . .

D.: She's never seen me. I've seen her, though.

A.G.K.: He says that you only are a witch.

G.: Huh?

A.G.K.: You're the only one. You're the only witch.

G.: No! He's a sorcerer!

A.G.K.: Did you ever see him [in a supernatural form] at
some time?

G.: Huh?

A.G.K.: Did you ever see him at some time?

G.: No. I've never seen him. I know he is a sorcerer because
this dog attacks him. He [the dog] would seize him if he were left
alone. Dogs don't like sorcerers. The dog leaves other people alone
—only him! He's a sorcerer!

Materia Medica

The medico-religious writings of the Cherokees would appear
to constitute the largest extant corpus of American Indian literature. Very few of these manuscripts have been translated, and even
fewer have been published.

Although some conjurations are, of course, known but to the
medicine men, any layman is likely to be able to say a charm
appropriate to some such minor emergency as a burn, a cut, or a

toothache. The following short example of such was obtained from a housewife in Stilwell.

Conjuration for Healing a Burn

This is what I used[12] to do to heal a burn: I used water, and this is what I said:

"Ice has been brought by the Anidawehi.[13]
Snow has been brought by the Anidawehi.
[Frost has been brought by the Anidawehi.
Dew has been brought by the Anidawehi.[14]]
They quickly make it feel cool.
Let the heat disappear into a very old tree."[15]
That's all.

Gatey'

What Even Poe Didn't Know

The belief in the Ravenmocker, the witch or wizard who changes into a raven for the purpose of gaining access to the bedside of someone ill and stealing that person's life-force, is dealt with in MMOC (pp. 401-3, 504-5). Among the tribal conservatives elaborate precautions are still taken to protect the ailing from a visit by a *kôlûn'ayelisgi* ("raven-imitator").

We append a transcription of the testimony of an old woman appertaining to a witch who commuted nightly from Oklahoma to North Carolina.

Gahnô and the Ravenmocker

GAHNO: That's what she did: just at sunset she went by, and she made cawing sounds. She wasn't flying over very high. She just whizzed by. Just at dawn, when it was becoming light, she flew back by. If one was awake at that time, one could hear her. And she disappeared in that direction [west]. She was a *kôlûn'*.[16] That's all.

ANNA G. KILPATRICK: What is a *kôlûn'*? What did you say it looked like?

G.: Did you say a kôlûn'? You see, we didn't actually see her because she passed at night when it was dark, and then she returned before it was light.

A.G.K.: Where did she go?

G.: What did you say?

A.G.K.: Where did she go when she passed?

G.: Well, there was an elderly person in the direction from which she was coming, and they said she was an adawehi,[17] and they said that that's who it was. This person had come from the Old Cherokee Country. She was . . .

A.G.K.: Yes. Where did she go then?

G.: Huh?

A.G.K.: Where did she go when she went by?

G.: I suppose she went back where she had come from in the Old Cherokee Country. She went back by before daylight. She didn't live very far from our home. She was a very old person. She had come from the Old Cherokee Country. She was living with one of her children.

A.G.K.: What was her name?

G.: Do you mean the old woman?

A.G.K.: Yes, the old woman. What was her name?

G.: Gagitlôsg'[18] was her name. Gagitlôsg'.

A.G.K.: What was her name in English?

G.: I don't know what her name in English was.[19]

Doi Delineates the Devil

We do not know whether Dôi can read English or not, but if he can, we are serenely confident of his innocence of John Milton. But he is a churchman, albeit rumor has it that he directed his thoughts above late in life. He experienced an urge to put his concepts of the Devil on record, minus a prerecording equation of that being with strong drink.

Dôi on Satan

Now [signifying readiness to begin]! This Satan that now lives on earth, a long time he and God were friends. He helped God by doing his work for him. They loved each other.

One day they disagreed. They got into a fight and had a war up there in Heaven. Satan was pushed out of Heaven and told never to come back. That's the reason he is around here. He once was loved and allowed to do anything he wanted to do.

My speech is not very good. It is because I had that stroke. I'm not speaking very well, I know, but I hope you can understand. But that's all [the best] I can do.

Dôi

A Small Gathering of the Clans

The exceedingly complex clan system has all but disappeared in Oklahoma, yet one still finds individuals who know their clan affiliation. Gilbert in GTEC has written an excellent monograph on clan relationships in North Carolina; we know of nothing comparable for the Western Cherokees.

The translation of the name of Dôi's clan, the Anigilôh', incidentally, has baffled every authority that has written about it. It has been mistranslated "Twisters" or "Long Hairs," or perhaps has been considered untranslatable. Cherokees whoop with merriment at "Twisters" or "Long Hairs"; for the word means "They Just Became Offended." The Anigilôh' clansmen still have a folk-reputation for touchiness and temper.

The Seven Clans

ANNA G. KILPATRICK: I wonder where we Cherokees came from. Did you ever hear?

DOI: We came from the Old Cherokee Nation[20]—that's where we came from.

A.G.K.: I mean before that.

D.: It is not known.

A friend of mine told me that back in the Old Cherokee Nation there is a town down in a valley, a deep valley. They call it *Chero-kee City. Cherokee City.*[21]

A.G.K.: That's true.

D.: And that is the Old Cherokee Nation.

A.G.K.: I see.

D.: The mountains are very high, and those people are our *kinfolks.* They are the ûgayû people. Do you know what ûgayû means?

A.G.K.: No.

D.: Seven-clan Society, they say. Seven-clan ûgayû. My clan is the Anigilôh'.

A.G.K.: I see.

D.: Mine is the Anigilôh'. And yours? Are you an Aniwôd'?[22]

A.G.K. (misunderstanding): Did you mean Anisûnôi?[23] Yes.

D.: They call them Nighthawks. They have seats here and there for the *Seven-clan Society* to sit upon.

A.G.K.: Did you say *Seven-clan Society?*

D.: Yes, that's it. Yes, that's it. You get it [clan affiliation] from your mother's side [of your inheritance].[24]

"Amazing How Friendly"

To most of the Oklahoma Cherokees, perhaps, their relatives in North Carolina (see GCNC, *passim*) are as remote as the Nepalese. But they cast many a thought backward to the "Old Cherokee Country" from which their tradition tells them that they were driven.

This interest also operates in reverse. We remember the touching inquiry of one old North Carolina Cherokee, the historic persecutions of his own group uppermost in his consciousness, "How are our people getting along in the West? Do they treat our people well?" It was beyond his understanding why all of the

Oklahoma Cherokees, now that the bitter days of the Removal were long since past, did not come back home.

Dôi's informant did not overstate the case for the friendliness of those eastern kinfolk. Our personal experience has convinced us that it is one of the most beautiful things still left in the world.

Dôi on the Eastern Cherokees

DOI: Sat'ki,[25] *near kinfolks* [there follows a word here that is indistinguishable] . . . this boy Sat'ki I was talking about. These Cherokees live away on top of the mountains, he said. They speak a very peculiar language, he said. They do not speak well; their speech is odd.[26]

"If you go up the hill, there you see a house," he said. "It's amazing how friendly they are. When you arrive there, they say, 'You're going home with me. I live over there'; and another one will say, 'No! You're going home with me! I live just over here.' They kept saying, 'I live over there. You come with me!' They all wanted me at the same time. 'Come with me!' 'Come with me! I live just right here!' Then another one would say, 'You come with me. I live right over that way.' They all wanted me. They are very friendly."

ANNA G. KILPATRICK: True!

D.: Away up the hill they will have a cornfield and a garden.

A.G.K.: Away up the hill.

D.: Yes. On the hill.

A.G.K.: True. We have been there. That's the way it [the situation] is.

D.: Another name for this Cherokee country is *Blue Mountain*.[27]

A.G.K.: *Blue Mountain?*

D.: Yes.

A.G.K.: The mountains are very high there. It [their custom] is not like the way you [Oklahoma Cherokees] have your gardens. They have their gardens away up on the hill.[28]

D.: Is that so?

A.G.K.: Yes. They don't have much *flat* land.

D.: Yes. That's what he said.

A.G.K.: Who was this that told you that?

D.: *His name was Fourkiller.* He had been there. His name is *James Fourkiller.* He had been there.

A.G.K.: That is true. They call it [the town on the Reservation] *Cherokee.*

D.: He is the husband of Dalala's[29] grandmother, and her name is Wat'.

Epithalamium

The marriage customs of Asudi's people were, and still are, characteristically devoid of sentimentality and ceremony. Cherokees have a pronounced tendency to underplay those very pivotal points in life that provide the white man with much-prized opportunity for display.

Asudi on Old-time Marriage

But the children who grow up and have children before they are grown—it used to be that they had to be twenty-one years old before they were considered grown. They didn't have marriage as it is today. If a man asked for the daughter, and he was given the daughter, they were encouraged to make their marriage endure, and they were helped by the people. They had to be of age—they had to be twenty-one years old, and that's when they could have a home, helped by others.

They [those in the community] gave them everything with which to begin. He didn't have to work all by himself at first. They showed him where he could find what he needed, and to the woman they gave quilts, and they showed her how to make a quilt. Indian women were always quilting.

Asudi

Of Rattles and Rattlers

The literature abounds in references to the traditional reverence of our people for the rattlesnake, an attitude that is much
decayed in Oklahoma. We recall one old gentleman, an herbalist,
who pointed out to us rattlesnake dens in the rocky hillside behind
his cabin near Gitahya Tl'gû.[30]

"I wouldn't harm one," he said of his dangerous neighbors.
"When I meet one in the path, I just tell it go away."

We have the opposite point of view represented here, however,
and by a man of equally conservative bent.

The terrapin-shell rattles of which he speaks were once used in
stomp dancing. The conversation concerning them was brought
on by our observing a pair displayed in his home.

This same individual, by the way, can still make one of those
bows that in the early days of contact with the white man elicited
this estimate: "They [the Cherokees] make perhaps the finest bows,
and the smoothest barbed arrows, of all mankind."[31]

On Terrapin-Shell Rattles

ANNA G. KILPATRICK: How do you fix those [terrapin-shell
rattles] when you make them?

AHAMA: I used a knife to take out the inside. After it [the
shell] dries, I put two or three marbles in it, and then I tie the
sides.

A.G.K.: How do you close [fasten] it?

A.: I tie it. I tie it with a wire. I put it [the wire] through
[the holes made to receive it] once, and then I twist it. When it
[the shell] dries, then it looks as these two look.

On Rattlesnakes

AHAMA: When I skin a snake, I first hang it up on a tree. I
skin its head first. I take off the skin from the top to the bottom.
After one begins pulling the skin off from the head, it [the entire
operation] is very easy. The outer part just slides off.

I killed one over at the late Uwôsôd' 's[32] place about twelve years ago that was seven feet four inches long, and it was eleven inches across the widest place on the skin.

ANNA G. KILPATRICK: What kind [of snake] was it?

A.: Rattlesnake.

A.G.K.: *Rattlesnake. Diamond rattlesnake.*

A.: Yes, that's right. *Diamond rattlesnake.* We were walking on the road. *Alex Sunday* was the foreman.

GATEY' (banteringly): He took the snake away from you, didn't he?

A.: When I brought it over to where they [the group of workers] were, *Alex Sunday*, the foreman, asked me for it. I gave it to him—or, he took it away from me! (General laughter.)

That's all I know. I don't know very much.

"Short and Simple Annals"

We cannot be certain to what tribal crisis the speaker was referring when he made the ensuing statement. Several well-documented occasions (*circa* turn of the century?) seemingly would fit. What he really had in view is relatively unimportant; all the interest lies in the insight into the patriarchal mind of the storyteller himself.

Asudi Remembers Famine and Strife

ASUDI: In the olden times when it snowed and it became bitter cold in the summertime[33] and the snow was that [demonstrating] high and the corn was that [demonstrating] high and it disappeared [was destroyed],[34] misfortune was coming. That's what the old people used to say. Those who had corn stored did not want to give any of it away. Some of them went off to hunt corn, some of them died, and some of them lived upon a small amount and survived. Tragedy was walking upon the earth in those days.

The late Diganôtsûhl'agayûl'[35] lived right over here [pointing].

That was his home there. They called him then, and he got ready to go. He called for five different tribes of brown people,[36] and he told them where to meet. He told them to go to Uwet' Disô'yû[37] for a meeting at Wadulisi.[38]

"Now we're going to get ready," he told them. "They want to take our land away from us. Let's go and fight for it. We're going to strive until our blood pours out," he told them.

Yes, they had the meeting, and they fought for their land until their blood poured out. God helped them, and they won. And that is the way it was. Those are all the events that I remember.

"A Big Fire In The Center . . ."

In this vignette we see extreme old age painfully searching back through three-quarters of a century of Christian serenity for the throb of the drum and the lilt of the spirit of pagan Youth.

Asudi on Dancing

ASUDI: I used to sing.

ANNA G. KILPATRICK: Can you remember a little?

SIQUANID': I think it [the song under discussion] used to sound like a hoot owl at night, and then it sounded like a fox. It was really a beautiful sound!

A.: Tsunihyûsdetsû![39]

S.: Yes.

A.:

Ha yu wa ni   ha yu wa ni   ya li ha yo

ya ni   ha yu wa ni   ya ne!

Ha yu wa ni   ga yu wi ni   ga yo ya ni

ga yu wa ni   ga ni!   Di- li- de- gô

ni- ga- we- sgô   sû- nô- yi   a-   di- sgô

Di- li- de- gô   ni- ga- we- sgô

sû- nô- yi   ni- ga we- sgô!   Ya na yo

ya na   ho   wi

ya na yo   ya na hi   ya na wi

ya   na yu!   Di- li- de- gô

ni- ga- we- sgô   sû- nô-   yi

a- di- sgô! Ti- ta- ga- de ni- ga- we- sgô

hu- git'- ste a- di- sgô! A- yû- squô

ni- ga- wa- sgô ya- na- hi yû- wa- li- hi.

Ya na no yû- wa- li- hi! Yo![40]

The late Lawûn' Dôi,[41] the dance-caller, was a Creek. And was he good! It was just amazing how he could start it [the dance]. But I have simply forgotten what he used to say when he started it. I used to know, because I used to be one of those dance-callers, but now I have forgotten what those Creeks used to sing. Some of them came from there [the Creek Nation], and others grew up here and just died here. But Lawûn' was born on the other side [the pre-Removal Creek country of the Southeast?]. They used to perform beautifully,[42] and you could hear the turtle shells rattling: "Sô! Sô! Sô! Sô! Sô! Sô! Sô! Sô! Sô!"

A.G.K.: And they had a big fire in the center . . .

A.: Yes! And the people used to dance around the fire. Well, I have just forgotten how they began; I just can't remember anything [about it] . . . The yell-leader started calling, and he continued on, and when he got through with his call, then they all followed him, and finally they danced with their partners. When they held their partners' hands, they went around the various areas [in the dance ground], and when they returned from dancing around the areas, they would quit. Sometimes they stopped at other places; sometimes they would dismiss the dance away from the fire. When the circle was as large as this [the yard], they would end the dance over there [demonstrating] somewhere. Now there were many that joined the dance. They were just thick.

O Tempora!

A nonagenarian, one would think, should be entitled to a certain lack of sympathy with the mores of the present; but Asudi's strictures on the younger generations do not stem from the sickbed philosophy of doddering senility, but rather from the keen observation of a man hale and in full possession of his faculties. Amazingly well-preserved physically (he might be mistaken for a man of sixty), Asudi has lost but little of his sensitive and sharp mental endowment. Unaffected but wise, devout yet understanding, open yet still reserved, in his green old age he symbolizes the national concept of the fruition of the good life.

Asudi on the Times

Long ago, when I was about eight or ten years old, I realized what it [life] was [all] about. At that time I heard all this talking. People came from away off to talk about these things. They [Asudi's parents] had many acquaintances, and these people came here [to the parental home] and exchanged stories. They didn't know sleep. All night and all day, the only time they lost was when they were eating. They spent their time talking about what was going to happen to them.

They said, "Our grandchildren will be in a very sad state. We won't be able to help them. We will be resting under the ground. We will not be able to do anything for them," they said.

And that is the way it is.

Then they said, "All the people will be talking, just mixing up words and not saying anything, and families will not have any love for each other." That's what they said. "Neighbors will not love one another. But we feel sorry for our people," they said.

And nowdays, just as God planned, men die. A long time ago, when men died, there was respect and silence for about a week; but nowdays, just as soon as they bury a man, they will start having a good time.[43]

It is amazing how things are nowdays and the way people are behaving, and if one would take notice of these things, one would know [what I mean]. People are doing so many [evil] things now, and also they are experiencing tragic times. They are just as bad off as they can be.

They go where there is no work, and something happens to them there. And those who stay quietly at home, they live longer. They see the next day again, and they can spend a whole day. But those that are on the road, they meet many disasters.

They foretold all of these things; they said that these things would be happening to people. Those who were traveling on the highways and those who went where there was no work, they said that these would meet disasters. That's what these old people said would happen, and that's what has happened to them. It is very sad—and it isn't good anywhere.

Those who stayed quietly at home, they're doing very well, and their minds are at ease, and they are happy. And the reason is, they allowed God to guide them. And those who didn't believe and went away met all these disasters. That's the reason why everything is in a bad condition and man is in such a sorry state.

Every day, every night, all day long and all night long, all week, they go without sleep; and those who do without sleep, the next day they meet with disaster. And that's the way it is. It's all because they do not believe in God—and they suffer for it. And those who believe, wake up in peace.

That's the way it is. It's amazing how it is. It's amazing what there is to tell.

Just as we are here, it's amazing how things will ring at times. Then it is quiet, and the only thing we can feel is the wind, a cool wind. Then it gets warm. Then late in the afternoon, it becomes cool. One never knows what is going to happen next.[44]

Asudi

The Cherokee Nostradamus

An adequate treatment of Cherokee divination would perhaps necessitate a whole book. The significant thing here is that Asudi, to our knowledge, makes no pretense to occult powers. He is not a shaman, nor presumably were the "old people" to whom he alluded. He is merely the possessor of that sensitivity to the adumbration of future events that plays a major role in the life of the average Cherokee layman.

Asudi on Cherokee Prophecy

ASUDI: All of these people used to talk about old times, what used to be, and also about what the future would be, and what they predicted is right on us now. They said that the Cherokees would be divided into two groups or perhaps three, whereas they used to have one government.[45] And it is really the way they said it would be. They never made any mistakes: what they predicted is coming true. That's what they said.

ANNA G. KILPATRICK: They knew what was going to happen, didn't they?

A.: Yes, they did. They knew it, just like [as definitely as] this thing [the tape recorder] talks; and what the radio reports is no different from what they predicted. Then they talked about things that were going to appear. They said that we were going [to be able] to hear people talking away off.

I wonder why. It's amazing, isn't it?

A.G.K.: It's amazing that they knew that.

A.: It's amazing.

I've been thinking since some time ago that somebody was coming while I was sitting around, and I was on watch. And you really did come. But, you see, I didn't know when.[46] I had been given something to foretell your coming. I knew that there was going to be somebody who was seeking something, and I was wondering what it was going to be. I just couldn't guess. And that's the way it was: you came to find out something.

A.G.K.: In olden times the Cherokee could foretell things, couldn't they?

A.: Yes, they could foretell. Yes, they could do it very well. They were told these things.

The Sacred Fire, the Sacred Art

Raymond D. Fogelson in FGSC (pp. 219-20) is referring to the Eastern Cherokees, but what he writes to a large extent holds true for the Oklahoma group: "As far as can be ascertained, all of today's conjurers consider themselves to be good Christians and feel that their work is completely consistent with Christian doctrine. The importance of faith and the power of prayer are fully recognized by the conjurer."

You will note that Asudi's hypothesis is that nowadays the pagan medicine is ineffective because practitioner and patient are not good enough Christians, and that the only recourse remaining is the even more ineffectual medicine of the white man!

Asudi on Fire and Medicine

When they [human beings] obtained fire, it was God's idea. When the white man came, he brought the match.[47] They [the Cherokees] used to use flint and dawôl'[48] in making fire. They used to have a large pile of dawôl' and flint. That's the way they had it [in a pile]. They used to need to strike just once to get a warm fire. There is a great difference between this fire and one made with a match. The match-fire is white; the flint-fire is red— a very good fire. That is the difference. They are different—a great deal.[49]

They used flint-and-dawôl' fire for medicine. They used it to warm [warm applications]. If they needed a great deal of medicine, that's what they used. They used to have round, legged pots, this size [demonstrating]. They used to make their fire out away from the house. They built it before the sun was up. They made this medicine, and it was finished by the time the sun was up. Then they used to empty it into containers. They could make the kind of medicine that was to be used to bathe the sick in or for them [the sick] to drink. That's the way that they made this medicine.

They always believed in God's Word, but nowdays they don't. They are now using other people's medicine. Most of it is no good; it doesn't work; it doesn't do what it is supposed to do. We are in a very bad way.

That's all I know. This is just the way I have heard what has happened here on earth. That's the way it is.

Asudi

Portrait of an Earnest Man

It is quite evident that an overwhelming majority of the Oklahoma Cherokees profess Christianity, although we cannot remember ever having seen any statistics to prove that they do. One gets the impression that the first missionaries to our people, once they solved the problem of communication (by teaching Cherokees English rather than by mastering Cherokee themselves) had a comparatively easy task. Yet, knowing the national sales-resistance as we do, the mock-serious statement that a native minister made to us gives one something to ponder. "The thing that bothers me," said he, "is how they ever converted the first Cherokee."

These mountain people study the Scriptures and appraise sermons with a Scottish earnestness. And these sermons can be surpassing materpieces of eloquence, logic, and poetry. The little rural churches have long been foci of community life. Still, one finds little that has been written concerning individual views, such as this one, on Christianity.

Asudi on Christianity

They talk [i.e., preach] about everything that God has made, and that's what I follow [spiritually]. You cannot make all in one [i.e., reconcile] everything as it is and all the books [religious books] that are printed. If you read from different sections of the Book, they would not all mean the same. It can't be the same. I wonder why it is that way.

A man named Uhyalug'[50] who grew up in this area,[51] who was born here, lived over there [demonstrating]. He was a preacher. We talked a lot. He used to say to me, "I cannot figure out the meaning of this Book. I don't know what it should mean in the end."

"I can't help you because I am just the same way [confused]," I told him. "If you can believe what is written and look up to God, you can get your best [clearest] meaning," I told him.

"That's what I believe," he used to say. And he was a preacher. I liked to talk with him. Everything that the people want or desire came from that beginning.[52]

HISTORICAL SKETCHES

ᏒᏫᏬ ᎵᎵ ᏒᎠᏲᏙ ᏒᏫᏬ

"Sequoyah. Yes, just Sequoyah."

HISTORICAL SKETCHES

OF GUNS AND A GHOST

The history of the Cherokees' occupancy of Oklahoma soil is a relatively short one, and there are those still living who, by means of the offices of the memories of their grandparents, can bridge its entire span. The small bulk of that history is shot through with tension of such power as to create the illusion of mass. For when the Cherokees came to rest in the West, they were an aggrieved, edgy, divided people beset by daily choices laden with eternal consequences.

The flash of outlaw guns and Cherokee steel thrust into Cherokee flesh in the fierce little fights of the Civil War were but fist-shakings at the lowering skies of Destiny, and the message of the little lame man rang above the snarling of feud-guns and outshone the glint of bayonets. For Sequoyah was not just a speck in Time, but a Voice that began when the first Cherokee sang to the sun and the soil his joy in something eternally apart from that of all other men.

Secret Weapons

Somehow one gets the impression that the soldiers referred to here were those of the First Indian Home Guard of the Union Indian Brigade, a regiment composed of Creeks with the exception of one company of Seminoles and another of Yuchis. The other two regiments in the brigade were Cherokees.

The curious statement that the narrator makes here to the effect that there was a war "from 1861 to 1863" may by no means be due to a slip in memory or to misinformation. By 1863 the Cherokee Nation was pretty well pacified (devastated might be

167

a more appropriate word) and in the firm possession of the Union forces, although, to be sure, there was some fighting subsequent to this. (See BUIB, *passim*.)

The Marching Creeks

From 1861 to 1863 there was a war. The Creeks were carrying these things: the scales from an Uk'ten'[1] and the uwôd'[2] from the lizard.

Now in this war the Creeks were being helped by these; they were carrying these things to help them.[3] That's the reason why they could not be put in the front [of the marching order]. They were always put in the rear. They marched in the rear.

Since they were carrying these things, if they were put in the front, they would go too fast and tire everybody in the rear. That's the reason why during the war they were put in the back.

That's all I know about this.

Yan'sa

"People Say You're Lookin' Back"

Galûts' and his wife Dadayi were sitting upon the porch of their cabin, reminiscing in the summer sundown, when we took this tape of the good life in the old Cherokee Nation. It is a sincere and moving record of the burnings in a human heart, and is as revelatory of the ones who spoke it as of the subject matter of their speaking. It is, moreover, an intimate glimpse of Cherokee economic concepts.

The Prosperity of the Old Days

GALUTS': We talk about how the woods used to be long ago. Acorns used to cover the ground. There were huge oak trees, and acorns were thick out in the woods. People won't believe that if you tell them nowadays, but that's the way it was. The trees were huge, and the ground in wintertime was covered. *That was mast in the woods, 'way years ago.* If you tell this to the white people, they won't believe it.

And when people wanted to fatten their hogs, they just let them live in the woods, and they would return home as fat as could be. They would come in about Christmastime, and they [the owners] would put them up in a pen for about two weeks. Then for those two weeks they would feed them [the hogs] corn and slop. They [the owners] would kill about ten or fifteen hogs at a time, and they had a great pile of meat. Nowdays you have to fatten them with corn, but in those days they used acorns. All summer long they fed out in the woods.

DADAYI: And nowdays if your hog goes into the woods, it'll be stolen! (Laugh.)

G.: Yes, if they found your hog anywhere, they'd steal it!

It was astonishing, and people say you're *lookin' back. The times was good 'way years ago. The mast in the woods was that* [demonstrating] *deep all over the country because we had the timber to raise that, you see. And the hogs would get out* [range]; *you didn't have to feed 'em.*

And cows and horses were the same. They had many horses. They were all well-to-do, even the womenfolk. They'd have as many as forty horses, and many cows. And they sold their hogs for five dollars apiece, sold their horses for ten or fifteen dollars—and the cows for the same.

There was a woman named Hayan' who lived over there [demonstrating]. She had to call on Uwôsôd⁴⁴ to count her money. She had three thousand dollars, and she charged only fifteen or twenty-five dollars for her horses, and the cows the same—five, ten, fifteen dollars (large cows)—and she accumulated that by selling those things.

I think this Hayan' was a relative of yours [of Anna G. Kilpatrick].

D.: I think she was your great-grandmother.

ANNA G. KILPATRICK: Was she my grandmother's mother?

G.: Yes, that's what she was. She was your grandmother's mother. Her name was Hayan'.

D.: Your grandmother's name was Wat' and Hayan' was her mother's name.

G.: Yes. They were well-to-do—and they didn't have a large acreage.

D.: They had many horses in the woods.

G.: That's the way people lived in those days.

D.: My grandfather had about the same thing [the same economic resources].

G.: That's the way people were in that day and time. They had many horses and many cows. Most of the Cherokees lived that way. If they had a home, they always had much livestock. And there's no telling how much money they counted. Three or four thousand dollars were counted for Nel' Hayan'[5] and her mother. Uwôsôd'[6] said that when he emptied out the money to count it, it was a great pile.

A.G.K.: Who did the counting?

G.: The late Uwôsôd'. It must have been about three or four thousand dollars that he counted for Nel' Hayan'. The mother [Hayan'] had even more. When they counted the money, they put it into a bag and tied it up. They counted by fifty's, and they would put fifty dollars in a bag and tie it. He had a very great pile of money when he was counting the money, said the late Uwôsôd'. Some white man was helping him count it, and the white man's eyes grew large.

D.: He probably wanted to come back that night! (Laugh.)

G.: No. It was night when they were counting it. It was astonishing how much money they had.

It is said that your great-grandmother sometimes threw old things away. The [some] children found an old purse that she had thrown away, and in it was a hundred-dollar bill. There's no telling how long it had been outside when they found it. When they [the parents of the children?] returned quite some time later, they found the children playing with the hundred-dollar bill which had been outdoors a long time. And I guess they took it! (Laugh.)

A.G.K.: They had quite a lot of money in those days.

G.: Yes, that's the way they were [wealthy]. You would have thought when you saw them that they were poor. They just sold eggs, horses, and cattle for five, ten, or twenty-five dollars. That's all that people paid in those days. But that's how they [the sellers] accumulated their money.

A.G.K.: I wonder what her [Hayan' 's] maiden name was [in English].

G.: I don't know.

A.G.K.: Was it P——?

G.: Yes, that's what it was. I don't know what their [Hayan' 's and Nel' 's] first names were.

That's the kind of old people we had in those days. You couldn't have told just by looking at them how well-to-do people were in those days.

Some people look back and say that those were the good old days. I look back, too; I look back to those *good times. And it was good times* in those days. People had an easy living. The Indians were left alone in the woods where they had all these things. And when the sawmills came, *well, they done away with all the timber, you see, and* [we] *don't have the mast.* The sawmills did that.

A Backyard Adventure

The country store type of yarn of some a-bit-out-of-the-ordinary personal experience is well represented in Indian oral traditions. And it appears to have that universal tendency to gather dimensions as it progresses from mouth to mouth. This specimen, coming as it does from the source, is of but modest size and shock-power. If it points up anything at all, it is one of the most engaging of tribal traits, the ability of the individual to laugh at his own misadventures.

The Lost Hunters

This that I wanted to tell you, I'll tell you now.

There was an old man named Uwedasat'.[7] He lived on the other side of the river [the Illinois], and he had an exceptionally good hunting dog. His dog's name was Kanûnô,[8] and he [Kanûnô] was an extraordinarily good possum hunter. He would tree coons.

I also owned a dog. They [this dog and Kanûnô] knew each other, and they were about the same size. He [the narrator's dog] was a possum and coon hunter.

One night, after a rain, it was still a little cloudy. "Let's go hunting tonight," Uwedasat' said. So we went hunting. We came through that [indicating] valley across the river. We had a lantern and a gun with us, and an ax.

After a while we had about three possums. The dogs were hunting less and we were just walking. "Well, I guess we had better go home," said old man Uwedasat'. (I was just a small boy, about thirteen years old.)

When we started toward his home, we walked down the valley toward his house. We lost our way. We had told them [the families of the hunters] that we would be back by nine o'clock. We couldn't find the road. We kept turning, searching around, and each time that we turned, we kept walking into brush. Then if we turned another way, we walked into more brush. We just kept getting into the brush.

"What shall we do?" said the old man—and I was wondering, too! Also, the dogs quit hunting, and I was beginning to get sleepy. The old man wasn't sleepy at all. Right beside us were briars, thorny ones, and there were berries upon them that look like huckleberries, but these ripen in the fall.[9] As we walked, we came into very dense brush and [an area of] huge rocks. We thought we were near home, but I guess we weren't.

"I suppose we'll just have to spend the night here," said the old man. "You hang that lantern upon a limb."

So I hung the lantern upon a limb, and the dogs made their beds nearby. They were sleeping right by a huge rock. Afterward the dogs got up and disappeared around that big rock, but they

returned soon, came back, and nuzzled us. Then again they disappeared and returned soon. We decided that we were too far
away from home [to continue searching], made our beds, and went
to sleep.

Early in the morning I awoke and heard a rooster crowing
somewhere. The crowing sounded far away. When I became wide
awake, I woke up old man Uwedasat'. I told him, "I hear a rooster
crowing. There must be a house near us."

So we got up, looked around, and we didn't see any brush
around us. When we called our dogs, they came from the direction
of the creek bed. When we walked from that area, we discovered
that we had been in old man Uwedasat' 's own backyard! There
was quite a lot of brush around. That's how we had gotten lost.
So we had slept outdoors beside his house. And it was cold and
raw, too!

That's all I know. This [story] is really true. That's what he
[Uwedasat'] and I did.

Siquanid'

Cherokee Bill

The memory of the outlaws—Indian, Negro, white, and all
gradations in between—that troubled the Cherokee Nation in the
bad old days is kept green by innumerable legends and an oc-
casional personal recollection imbued, as often as not, with a somewhat legendary tint. Cherokee Bill was one of the most notorious
of the malefactors who, if local historians are to be credited, in-
dustriously sowed the hills of eastern Oklahoma with treasure
caches before falling afoul of Judge Isaac Parker, "the Hanging
Judge," and his Federal Court in Fort Smith, Arkansas (see
HCBO, *passim*).

Cherokee Bill was born Crawford Goldsby at historical old
Fort Concho near San Angelo, Texas, on February 8, 1876, and
he finished off his career on the gallows at the time and place re-

called with such vividness by Dalala (N.). He was just one-eighth
Cherokee; Sioux, Mexican, white, and Negro strains were also
represented in his ancestry.

This would appear to be the proper occasion for pointing out
that Cherokees are somewhat given to treasure-hunting, and that
Siquanid' is reputed to be a handy man with a spade himself.

Dalala (N.) Remembers Cherokee Bill

DALALA (N.): Yes, they hanged the late Cherokee Bill.[10] I remember it [the hanging] very well. Maybe you know about it,
too. I was thirteen or fourteen years old. He was hanged at Uwet'
Disôyû.[11] His name was Cherokee Bill.

ANNA G. KILPATRICK: Was he hanged?

D.: Yes, he was hanged, and I was in jail there at the same time.
We were in at the same time. That's what I will tell about.

A.G.K.: What was his name? Bill what?

D.: Cherokee Bill.

D.: On March 17, 1896, at ten o'clock in the morning, he was
hanged. That's all. I just thought I would tell this.

A.G.K.: Why was he hanged?

D.: He had killed seven people.[12] He was a bank robber and
a very wicked person.

A.G.K.: He was very wicked? And he was really a Cherokee?

D.: No, he was not all Cherokee. He was white, Negro, and a
small part Cherokee.

A.G.K.: He was part-Negro?

D.: Negro and white.

A.G.K.: Where did it [the crime for which he was hanged]
happen? Here around Stilwell?

D.: Squawahlisôdû.[13] I have a picture at home of the whole
group that took part in that [the murder of Earnest Melton].

A.G.K.: Do you have any old photographs?

D.: Just this one. Five of them [Cherokee Bill's gang]: one
was Wil' Adastayûhûsg',[14] the late Tsim' Adastayûhûsg',[15] the late

Galûts',[16] and a white man named Dos'.[17] That's the only photograph I have.

A.G.K.: Is that all?

D.: That's all. If one had more time, one could think up more things. All I remember is about Cherokee Bill: he is so well-known—and he was very wicked. He had killed seven people. Bank robber.

A.G.K.: They called him Cherokee Bill?

D.: Yes. Cherokee Bill. In appearance he looked more like a colored person, and his hair was very much like Negro hair. He was fairly good looking. He wasn't very dark in complexion, but he was freckled. His complexion was rather yellowish.

[The following is a transcription of a portion of a tape made a few days later than the above].

D.: What about Cherokee Bill? Does he [Jack F. Kilpatrick, who operated the recorder] have a recording of it [Dalala's reminiscence]?

A.G.K.: Yes, he has it. You told it the other day, didn't you?

D.: But he didn't play it back to me.

A.G.K.: But he recorded it—Cherokee Bill.

D.: Yes, I talked about Cherokee Bill. He was hanged in 1896— March 17. That's what I told you the other day.

A.G.K.: You were both in jail at the same time, weren't you?

D.: Yes. We were in there together.

A.G.K.: Why?

D.: I was accused of murder. My father, my brother, and I were all in there at the same time. But Cherokee Bill was already in there when we got in. Did you know of Henry Starr,[18] another bank robber? He was in jail, too, at that time.

A.G.K.: But you got out of it, didn't you?

D.: Yes. In four months and two weeks I got out. But my brother and father were in there seventeen months, and they were released.[19] Now he didn't get down what I said, did he?

A.G.K.: I think he did. (Laugh.)

D.: (Laughing) I rather mended my story since the last time
I told it!

A Legend of Cherokee Bill

There was a man named Gûtisût'[20] who lived over near where
Barber used to be.[21] A long time ago at Sycamore Tree Church[22]
there was a small house near the church, and that was where my
family and I lived, and my mother was living with us. There used
to be a man who came over there [to visit]. His name was Udisgatl'
Yonuwôi,[23] and he told me this later, about the doings of Cherokee
Bill when he was a bank robber.

The late Gûtisût' who lived on this [the south] side of
Uhyôdû[24] was very old and didn't have much time to live.
Udisgatl', who used to come to see me often, was a deacon in our
church, and that's why he used to come to see me and tell me often
of things that happened long ago.

And so Udisgatl' told me that the late Gûtisût' used to fish
often. So one day he went fishing, Gûtisût' told Udisgatl', and he
told me. At Unadiquanôst'[25] the road ran right up the hill, and you
traveled upon those hills that run right near Cookson.[26] Those hills
are [likewise] called Unadiquanôst', and the road goes downhill
there [at Cookson].

Gûtisût' went down the hill and came to what they call Atsinôwuwequatsû.[27] He arrived there at the place I called Atsinôwuwequatsû. There is a huge bluff there, and the water is directly
below it. This was the best place to fish. All of the old people used
to like to go there to fish because they could catch such huge fish
there, and the late Gûtisût' knew that, and he went there to fish.
When he arrived there, he didn't know the country beyond that;
he only knew that Atsinôwuwequatsû was a good place to fish.
He went there very often to fish.

And when he sat down to fish, he heard some persons talking.
He couldn't decide whether they were to the right or to the left
of him. Finally, after a while, he looked to the left of him and saw

in the sumac bushes four—I mean five—horses, all black, and some
persons who were very old, wearing huge hats, were saddling the
horses. He recognized one of them the instant he saw him. The
reason was, he knew him—a wicked bank robber who used to live
a long time ago. His name was Bill the Cherokee—some called him
Cherokee Bill—and there he was, saddling his horse, and Gûtisût'
recognized him instantly.[28]

When the rest of them mounted their horses, they all went
across the water to the left. When they all crossed, they disappeared
to the left into the woods.

The late Gûtisût' wondered about it; so he started off walking
and he kept looking in the direction in which they had disappeared.
He was wondering about Cherokee Bill's disappearance. He kept
thinking about the manner in which he had seen him, and he stared
at the place where Cherokee Bill had disappeared.

He got up and walked to where they [the outlaws] had been.
Where this little creek flowed into the river, there was a huge cave
about the size of a three-room house. They [the outlaws] had
fixed it up very prettily inside, and there were many various things
in there. They had stacked stones for chairs.

When he finished inspecting the place, he began to think about
it, and he went outside and got upon higher ground where the
surface was level. He looked down into the valley and saw in the
bushes a smooth path.

So he followed that path and went through a sumac thicket.
The path was just big [wide] enough for one person to go through,
but the path was worn smooth because they [the outlaws] had
gone through there every day.

When he got down into the valley, he lost his way because the
path ended there. Where the path ended, there was a hollow stump,
as tall as a man, with a side open. He peeped through the opening
into the stump, and when he looked in there, he saw a sack such as
they used a long time ago to put candy in, so that the candy
wouldn't spill out. That's the kind of sack that was in that stump.

It was sitting up straight. It was half-full of something. It was tied at the top, and the late Gûtisût' took hold of it where it was tied. It was so heavy that it was beyond his strength, but he finally got it out and set it on the outside.

When he put it outside, he was considering what he should do. He untied the sack and discovered when he untied it that it was full of gold pieces—all gold money.

And that was what Cherokee Bill had stolen. He robbed just about anything, even a train that was traveling at top speed. Cherokee Bill could do it, and if he had to do it alone, he did it. He even disconnected trains while they were in motion, they say, and when he disconnected one, that left one [coach] on the track, and that's the way he robbed people. That's how they [the outlaws] accumulated this money. The late Gûtisût' found the half-bagful.

He had a mule. He went to get it. He had it tied somewhere nearby. He had this mule to ride when he went fishing. He divided the money into two portions in the sack, and then put the sack upon the mule's back.

He traveled all day when he started from there. Unadiquanôst' ends at Cookson. The hill that comes straight down to Cookson is a large hill. Some call it Unuk'sutii.[29] The white people call it *Rattlesnake Inn*. They [Gûtisût' and the mule] went up this hill, whereas before he [Gûtisût'] had come down it.

Just as the road goes down the hill at Unadiquanôst', he took the money off the mule and set it down by a rock. He said, "Tomorrow I will put it away." He went on down the hill riding the mule.

Next morning he put it [the money] in an iron pot and counted it—sixty-five thousand dollars, said the late Udisgatl' who was told by the late Gûtisût'.

"Now I have the small amount of ten thousand dollars right over there where I can see with my eyes, about three-quarters of a mile away. To the northeast, a little more to the north than to the east, I have it hidden. This ten thousand dollars is for my everyday use." Gûtisût' was on his deathbed when he told this story to Udisgatl' who was caring for him. "I have hidden sixty-five thousand dollars just on top of the mountain which is by Unadiquanôst', and you get to this place by going by this path—as you go up the mountain, just this side of the top of the mountain.

"I have thought of this money as something for you, my sons, and for you in this household to live on after I am gone. And when you hunt for this money, don't use anything that is customarily used to hunt money. Use your eyesight. I have put up two stones, one on the north side and one on the south side of where the money is buried, and in the middle I have a large amount [of money]. Be sure to look for these two stones, and you will find the money in the middle," he told his sons, said Udisgatl', and he told me.

And when they went to look for this money, this sixty-five thousand dollars, they couldn't find it, and to this day nobody has been able to find it. The older men say that the money must still be there somewhere in the rocks. The late Udisgatl' told me that the late Gûtisût' did it [hid the money], because he was the only one who waited on this man until he died, and he had heard everything he said at the end. He told what he had heard this man say, and he used to go down there a lot to Atsinôwuwequatsû to fish, and that's where he found out these things.

That's all I know. That is just how long it [the story] is. There is always a lot that can be learned of the past by listening to these old people.

Siquanid'

"Sequoyah. Yes, Just Sequoyah"

The Cherokees revere the memory of Sequoyah as the greatest Cherokee that ever lived, and the farther his figure retreats into time, the larger his shadow falls across the present. To them he is much more than the genius who made them a literate people: he is the eternal symbol of the national virtues of wisdom, forbearance, and compassion.

By all standards Sequoyah was indeed one of the truly towering American Indians. It is highly significant that the national hero of the Cherokees was an intellectual, not a warrior.

Our people refuse to let him go, this small lame man who taught and led and loved them in their persecuted past. He has been enshrined in a Messianic mysticism that the essentially pragmatic Cherokees reserve for him alone. With shining eyes an old woman once said to us: "He will come back someday."

The mystery that beclouds his parentage, his birth, his name, his death somehow seems appropriate for a man who has completely passed into the spirit of his people.

Asudi on Sequoyah

ASUDI: When he wrote it [the Sequoyah syllabary], he began with one word; then he wrote it a second time, a third, fourth, fifth, sixth, seventh, eighth—and tenth time. The tenth was complete as far as understanding was concerned. That's the reason why we have written Cherokee. That's how *Sequoyah*[30] spoke [made communication]. He began with just one [syllable or word?]. All of the Bible that we have was spoken [communicated] by *Sequoyah*. That's where they obtained what they printed.

He lived sometime in the 1800's—1855.[31]

ANNA G. KILPATRICK: Did you say '55?

A.: Yes. He lived in 1855. After that—1860, '70, '80, '90—he lived right there [?].[32]

A.G.K.: And your father knew him?

A.: Yes.[33] My father's name was Esa Adaket'.[34]

A.G.K.: What was his name?

A.: Esa Adaket'.

A.G.K.: Esa Adaket'.

A.: Yes.

A.G.K.: Was he [Sequoyah] a full-blood Cherokee?

A.: Yes.[35]

A.G.K.: He didn't have any white blood?

A.: No. He could speak English.[36]

A.G.K.: He could speak English.

A.: He spoke English.

A.G.K.: But he was not part-white, was he?

A.: All Cherokee.[37]

A.G.K.: What was his real name? They don't really know what his name was. They say his name when they say Sequoyah in English was *George Guess.*[38]

A.: Yes. *Sequoyah.*

A.G.K.: I see.

A.: Yes. It was just *Sequoyah*[39] . . . *Sequoyah.* Yes, just *Sequoyah.* His last name I don't know.

A.G.K.: You don't?

A.: No. His name was just *Sequoyah.*

A.G.K.: I wonder if there are any living relatives?[40]

A.: No. There aren't any.[41]

A.G.K.: Aren't there any?

A.: No. He was the only one left. The others were all dead. He grew up an orphan. He grew up in this area.[42] He didn't come from anywhere else. That's where [demonstrating] he grew up, in Sequoyah County. He lived just on the other side of Ekûn',[43] just right near Ekûn'.

A.G.K.: Whom did he marry?[44]

A.: I don't know whom he married. They never did say. I don't know if he was married.

A.G.K.: I see.

A.: The only thing I know was that they said he lived alone a great deal.

A.G.K.: He lived alone?

A.: Yes. He didn't have any children.

A.G.K.: He didn't have any children?

A.: No. He was quite alone. Nobody knows where he was buried when he died.

A.G.K.: He died when he was away off somewhere, didn't he?

A.: That's what they say. And this is what they say: He and his children (he had been married, I suppose), two sons, started off and went toward the West, and away off they stopped, and when they stopped (they [his sons] went in a wagon and he upon a horse) he told them, "Over there is some corn. I want you to go get it." He told them that there was a wagonload of this corn over there in the southwest. When they left, he was there; when they returned, he was gone. They found the corn, a wagonload of it. When they returned with the wagonload, they couldn't find him, and they didn't know what to do to find him. He left and went to the West, they say when they tell it.

A.G.K.: I wonder what his name means. Some say, "Pig in a Pen."

A.: (Laughs)

A.G.K.: Sequoyah . . . what does it mean?

A.: I don't know.

A.G.K.: You don't?

A.: No. His name was *Sequoyah.*

A.G.K.: They used to say that his name originally meant "Pig in a Pen."

A.: No. That's not correct. His name was Siquoyi.[45] He was an average-sized man, not a large man.

A.G.K.: Did he use a cane?[46]

A.: I don't believe so. My father never told me that he used, or did not use, a cane. My father never talked about that.

A.G.K.: Your father didn't have any old books?

A.: No. He didn't have any. That's the way it was: he [Sequoyah] left, and nobody knows what became of him, they say.[47]

A.G.K.: He died out there [in the West] somewhere, didn't he?[48]

A.: I don't know. I believe he died here [in eastern Oklahoma]. When everything came to light, [it was revealed that] he really didn't disappear. They say he died far away. No! That's not so! My father said he died here. My father used to say this.[49]

A.G.K.: Your father said that he died here?

A.: Yes. Right here.

A.G.K.: Did he [Asudi's father] see him buried?

No, he didn't see him [buried]. He just knew [about] it. He didn't say whether he saw him or looked at him, but he had heard that he died here. He heard that he died, but he didn't know where or when they buried him. They don't know where [the exact site] he is buried. They talk about his burial place, and it is right on the other side [south of?] Salun'geyû.[50] There was a Choctaw who lived there. He had a cemetery. They say that he [Sequoyah] was buried in it. The Choctaw was a doctor [medicine man] who traveled about, but he lived there.

A.G.K.: What was his name?

A.: His name was Tsis'.[51] He lived near *Watson*.[52] He was the one who told me all these things that happened so long ago. And then over here at Tsuyôhusû[53] there was a man named Gadûgug' Nôqu's,[54] another one named Diyôhl',[55] and another named Gadudeg'[56]—all of these men went together to see him [after he died]. And there were some [men] from around Tahlequah (I lived there awhile, too)—they also came to see him.

NOTES

NOTES

THE STORYTELLERS

1. A curer. The Cherokees have several classes of "medicine men." A *didahnûwisg'* can be equated roughly with the white man's "doctor."

BIRD STORIES

1. The narrator employed the generic term for "bird" *(tsisqua)* to refer to one of the birds, but in shifting into English he got his specific birds confused.

2. This story makes the easy substitution of the Heron for the Crane.

3. From this point on the narrator moved back and forth from Cherokee to English in pronouncing the word "Hummingbird"—a personal idiosyncrasy of no particular moment.

ANIMAL STORIES

1. The Creek, Koasati, and Natchez Cherokee forms of this myth in SMTS give the appearance of being but variations on a Cherokee theme.

2. It was the opinion of the storyteller, and it is also ours, that these syllables are absolutely meaningless. They do not appear to form any words, archaic or otherwise, with the exception of *dil'*, which means "skunk."

3. Small lapses into English dotted Dôi's routine conversation as well as his storytelling.

4. Seven, the most sacred numeral of the Cherokees, makes its appearance in mythology with a frequency that one might well mistake for a lack of creative imagination.

5. Ka!—the Cherokee signal for starting a race, also used in other and similar circumstances.

6. This seems to be as good a place as any to consider the protean "hawa," a word that could mean, depending upon inflection, any number of things in the nature of "good," "all right," "very well," "I agree." We have usually translated it as "all right."

7. SMTS, p. 272.

8. Up to this point the story-line was quite clear; but for some reason the narrator concluded that he had botched his effort, and in attempting to mend it muddled matters rather sadly.

9. It is not clear here whether the King was the Supreme Ruler of the Universe or merely the monarch of the animals. *Ugûwiyuhi*, the word employed, is a troublesome one in Cherokee; for it could signify "Chief" as well as "King." The language of the incurably democratic Cherokees is singularly poor in terms that express political authority.

10. SMTS, pp. 208, 241.

11. MMOC, pp. 266-67.

12. Gilbert states in GTEC, p. 302, that this was one of nineteen myths that he collected in 1932 at Big Cove, Eastern Cherokee Reservation.

13. In MMOC the Rabbit sings his instructions. Unfortunately Mooney did not give us the music to which it was sung.

14. Our storyteller got his animals transposed.

15. BTSM, pp. 694-702.

16. MTS, p. 273.

17. In explanation of the nasal formation of the animal.

18. The buzzard as a symbol for the healing art was a widespread motif in the Southeast.

19. This story is in effect an "enigma variation": the theme, the Rabbit injuring himself trying to match the prowess of the bear, is never stated.

20. We encounter the motif of the testudinate archer again in "The Touchy Turtle and His Waspish Wife."

21. One of the authors recalls hearing this specific version from a Creek fellow student at Bacone College (at that time an institution exclusively for Indians) about 1934.

22. The significance of the color of the Crow's legs is far from clear. The Terrapin, of course, is excusing himself on grounds of poor eyesight.

23. This is the commonest Cherokee exclamation in response to a sudden sharp pain. The accent in the word is on the second syllable.

24. See note 22 *supra*.

25. An obvious *lapsus linguae*.

26. This unconscious substitution of the synonym for Tseg'sgin' in place of the name of Maneater supports the inference stated above.

27. SMTS, *passim*.

28. SEYI, p. 153.

29. This is exceedingly aberrant Cherokee, but it appears to mean "Run! He's fooling you."

30. "Choose the gobbler!" "Hasuyeg'" would be the commoner form for "you (second person, singular) choose it."

31. See the prefatory note to "Fireless Cookers."

32. Siquanid' inadvertently omitted the creatures in other categories.

33. A "gadug'" essentially is a group that donates labor to a worthy cause (*vide* GCAC, *passim*).

34. The Oklahoma Cherokees will say *"Gadug' dunisûstanei"* ("They called for a *gadug'* "). Depending upon the ensuing syllable, the word for a free-labor crew is sometimes pronounced "gadugi." It appears to be always so written in ethnological and sociological monographs.

35. The narrator must have forgotten having said previously that they tied his legs.

36. The correspondence in spirit here with the Biloxi version in DSOB, pp. 14-15, is noteworthy.

37. This would appear to be the first time that this story in a complete, or nearly complete, form has ever been taken down. One can now understand its *raison d'être*: it is a myth in explanation of the origin of rivers.

UK'TEN' STORIES

1. See "The Friendship of Thunder."

2. We find no English equivalent for this expression. As close as we can come to it, it would be: "One would fall to the ground with great force at some distance away."

3. See "Magic Is Wherever You Find It."

4. The Cherokees frequently refer to themselves and to other Indians as "brown" people (never "red").

5. Yan'sa had just finished telling his version of "Thunder and the Uk'ten'."

6. Presumably also the gift of the old man.

7. This uncharacteristic good will upon the part of the Uk'ten', not being elucidated in the story, opens speculation as to the possibility of an ellipsis.

8. The Tie-Snake of the Muskhogean peoples is roughly the equivalent of the Cherokeean Uk'ten', but minus much of the ferocity and most of the magical attributes of the latter.

9. Some of this rhapsodic repetition derived from Yan'sa's personal style of speaking; a part of it may have been due to his age.

10. A hearing on tape of the Yan'sa version elicited this display of professional courtesy. Out of deference to Yan'sa's age and reputation Siquanid' confesses the possible inferiority of his own way of telling the story; but he stoutly but tactfully defends its validity by reference to the unimpeachable purity of its source.

11. Cherokee concepts of a nomenclature for familial relationships are of singular complexity (*vide* GTEC, *passim*). In the interest of simplification, let us say that the term "nephew" implies ties far closer than in the European connotation.

TALES OF MONSTERS

1. OMSM, p. 12.

2. In his Glossary (p. 529), however, Mooney examines the etymology of the word and arrives at "Stone-clad."

3. What Asudi was referring to here is not clear to us.

4. Whether the large red hard-shelled ant that the Oklahoma Cherokees call *nûy'unuw'* is the same insect as the one similarly designated in North Carolina is a question that only a qualified myrmecologist could answer. The Oklahoma insect is *Dasymutilla occidentalis*.

5. Asudi must have meant that Stoneclad, though gigantic, was nevertheless of a size within the human frame of reference.

6. In the existing myths about him, he is represented as keeping quite busy—catching and eating human beings.

7. This view of Stoneclad as a somewhat dangerous but retiring eccentric who quietly faded away is in sharp contrast to the monster of the myths, a being whose extermination necessitated much effort and ingenuity. It leads one to wonder if in his youth, eighty years or so ago, Asudi had heard a quite dissimilar myth, or perhaps cycle of myths, that died with those who knew it.

8. We call your attention to the synoptic Creek story "The Big Rock Man" (SMTS, p. 38), almost certainly borrowed from the Cherokees.

9. *Vide* MMOC, p. 234; J.N.B. Hewitt, "Tawiskaron," in HHAI, II, 707-11.

10. MCIP, p. 67.

11. Despite radical divergences here from MMOC (pp. 274-75), there is retention of some pivotal parallels: Flint lived in the mountains—Flint announced that he would preach from a mountaintop; the Rabbit went to visit Flint—the Rabbit went to ascertain why Flint had not kept his word; the Rabbit destroyed Flint with a stake and mallet—the Rabbit destroyed Flint with a stick.

12. *Atsôsesgei*—trying to stave off sleep by fidgeting about.

13. With little or no jar to the consciousness one could substitute Stoneclad for

Flint in the first part of this myth, and the suspicion that someone did make such a transposition naturally arises. But since that of Flint which has come down to us is almost certainly vestigial, we cannot prove that Siquanid' has portrayed him out of character. One too readily remembers the female stoneclad cannibal in MMOC (pp. 316-19).

14. Tsuhl'gûl' means "they are slanting," referring, of course, to the eyes of this being. Also see MSFC, p. 341.

15. See the chapter on "Uk'ten' Stories."

16. It is very significant that Siquanid' spoke of a race of these creatures. Tsunihl'gûl' is the plural of Tsuhl'gûl'. This tale is quite different from the one in MMOC, and we have never heard it before, let alone seen it in print.

17. The "Old Cherokee country" at the time of first contact with Europeans embraces portions of Tennessee, North Carolina, South Carolina, Kentucky, Alabama, and Georgia.

18. This may refer to Tennessee Bald in Jackson County, North Carolina, upon which a Tsuhl'gûl' was reputed to live and have a farm (the "bald"). See MMOC, p. 407.

19. While not as sacred as the number seven, four is also sacrosanct.

20. Anidaweh'. These anidaweh' possess surpassing knowledge and ability.

21. Siquanid' corrected himself here.

22. A modern touch this! Tsat' is "choc" (or "chock"), otherwise known as "Choctaw beer," a revolting beverage of Prohibition days.

23. Previously the narrator had defined the capacity of one of these barrels as sixty-four gallons.

24. In the early historic period the Cherokees practiced sororal polygyny extensively (vide DMCS, chap. xvii, pp. 394-407).

25. SMTS, passim.

26. As egregious an error as exists about a people remarkable for having attracted misinterpretation is the statement, likely to be found even in sources that are almost universally considered to be beyond reproach, that the Cherokees call themselves "Aniyûwiya," the word that Yan'sa used here. The Cherokees call themselves "Anitsalagi." "Aniyûwiya" simply means "Indians," of any sort whatever. It is not a tribal name.

27. See the chapter dealing with this mythical creature.

28. "Charley To-Move-It"; "Charley He-Calls-Him."

29. Barber is a lakeside community on the east side and the upper end of Tenkiller Lake in Cherokee County.

30. This was the first sentence after a new roll of tape was put on the recorder; hence the repetition.

THE LITTLE PEOPLE

1. Standing Rock, a clifflike formation formerly overlooking a favorite fishing site on the Illinois River south of Tahlequah, is now a bluff above Tenkiller Lake not far from the State Highway 82 bridge.

2. The dam across the Illinois River at Tenkiller Ferry that impounds Tenkiller Lake.

3. The Cookson post office and store, now on State Highway 82 that follows up the east bank of Tenkiller Lake, at the period of Yan'sa's narrative was on the Illinois River and somewhat west of the present location.

4. "Daylight."

5. "Groundhog."

6. The Cherokee form of Standing Rock.

7. "Going Around Place"—a proper name.

8. "The Eternal Ones."

9. This narrator amended his preamble by pointing out that if the adventure took place in "this area," i.e., Oklahoma, then it was not, as he had said at first, "A long time ago—long, long ago."

10. "This Is the Way They Went."

11. "Pigeon."

12. A certain race of Little People, according to Cherokee belief, dwell in cliffs and rocky sites. The Eastern Cherokees have a term for this specific class of spirits, but we cannot recall having heard the word in Oklahoma. Cf. GTEC, p. 345, and WHCI, *passim*.

13. All of this adventure?

14. "One Who Walks About."

15. The whites also call this eastern Cherokee County community Sugar Mountain.

16. Caney Creek rises in the outskirts of Stilwell, in Adair County, and flows west through some of Oklahoma's loveliest terrain. It debouches into Tenkiller Lake at Caney Creek Cove.

17. There is something so typically Cherokeean about the lapidary nature of this sentence that we call your attention to it. This statement is redolent of the grammatical spice that grows only in Cherokeeia.

18. "Leaf."

19. "Spade."

20. *Yûw'usti.*

21. See the previous tale.

22. The stomp dance as a social institution is almost extinct among the Oklahoma Cherokees, and the younger folk evince little or no interest in resuscitating it. Oldsters point out with nostalgia sites, now likely as not under cultivation or retaken by forest, where the stomp dances of yesteryear were held.

23. That is, in their human manifestations.

24. *Dilaskahl't'.* There is a photograph of an Eastern Cherokee ball player holding a pair of *dilaskahl't'* in HHAI, I, 245, and there is also a drawing of these implements in *ibid.*, p. 251.

25. See "The Friendship of Thunder."

26. This explanatory paragraph raises new questions, of course; but such is what the narrator said. Consistency is not reckoned as a jewel by tellers of folktales.

27. The idiom *Dôhiyu kai* is a thorny one to translate. "Too bad" might be closer to the meaning.

28. MSFC, pp. 375-84; OMSM, pp. 154-55.

29. Throughout this preamble one senses a lack of certainty in the narrator's mind as to whether the Little People still exist, or merely once existed.

30. *Uhisôti* is a state of ecstatic yearning, an otherworldly melancholia, peculiarly Cherokeean. It is generally attributed to the sorcery of an enemy.

31. A free translation would run somewhat like this:

> I, the Little Person, just came from the Sunland.
> I speak well.

Who else can do as much as easily?
Let us tell them that I obtained my attire
From the Lightning,
Which is never lonely.
Di-gi-di-di-di!

32. "Fierce Charley."

33. Wise, powerful, capable of doing many things, both natural and supernatural.

34. This term does not appear to be translatable.

35. The young leaves of this plant (*Phytolacca decandra*) are consumed by both whites and Indians as a spring green. Portions of the plant are reputed to be narcotic, the seeds of the red berries to be poisonous.

36. A translation of this would be:

I am as beautiful
As the Red Tsugûtsalala.
When I am lonely
I stand beside them.
I believe that somewhere
You do the same for me.

37. This may be translated:

I am as beautiful
As the Red Rainbow.
From my feet on up
I am beautiful.

The color red would seem to be used in the ritualistic sense of "powerful, fortunate." In Cherokee symbolism red is the quintessence of everything that is desirable.

TSEG'SGIN' STORIES

1. The narrator actually employed the synonym for Tseg'sgin'—Tseg'nudan'tûn', "Brainless Jack."

2. This troublesome word for "Ruler" could mean "King," of course, but "Chief" seems to be contextually more appropriate.

3. SITN, pp. 190, 219.

4. SMTS, p. 1.

5. The narrator apparently forgot that she had had her hunter remove his shoes before he got into the water.

6. Tseg'nudan'tûn'.

7. This was probably a violin, although the Cherokee term was a generic one.

8. Tseg'nudan'tûn'.

9. The Cherokee expression is "family-man."

TALES OF HUMOR

1. A mortar made by hollowing out the end of a hardwood log. To a certain extent the *kanôn'* is still used.

2. Figure of speech for "wanted to marry her."

3. A dish made of cracked corn.

4. We call attention to the myth about the owl in OTBB, pp. 131-32.

MISCELLANEOUS STORIES

1. *Selu*.

2. *Newada*.

3. The inference is that she proposed to begin cooking at noon.

4. The meaning is, "No, we do not dislike you."

5. The Cherokee implies that the stick was suspended like the crosspiece in a hurdle. One might question how the Turtle broke off a piece of it by jumping "over" it, but the statement is explicit.

6. The literature is explicit in its separation of these entities. A careful recheck of the tape confirms this word-form.

7. *Ugûwiyuhi.*

8. The beasts were indavertently omitted.

9. We call especial attention to this statement.

10. This is a highly resistant belief in both branches of the nation.

11. Tsusgadigisg': "eater of heads."

ETHNOLOGICAL DATA

1. As a member of the household.

2. Elk Creek flows into upper Tenkiller Lake from the east at Elk Creek Landing.

3. The Cherokee language, marvelously precise in many ways, is a poor instrument with which to define felines; but for that matter, English, with its "panthers" and "bobcats" (the animals referred to), does no better.

4. This was in the old Sequoyah District of the Cherokee Nation.

5. "Smaller Creek." We do not know any English name for it.

6. Deer.

7. Jack Jumper.

8. For some reason Gahnô actually used here and following Dalala's English name, which for obvious reasons we do not wish to reveal.

9. The Cherokees believe that dogs can detect witches and sorcerers.

10. *Sûnôyi anedôhi.*

11. In a transformed state.

12. A stalwart Christian, the informant wants to be sure of leaving the right impression; therefore the statement that she "used to do" as described.

13. This is the plural of *adawehi*: a being, human or spiritual, possessed of superlative powers. As stated elsewhere, the human *adawehi* we translate as "conjurer."

14. Since we were already familiar with the conjuration, we have taken the liberty of inserting two lines omitted (perhaps intentionally) by the informant. Observe that the natural phenomena are listed in a descending order of degrees of coldness.

15. In other words, let the heat go into something of no value, i.e., "a very old tree."

16. Gahnô employed a contraction.

17. See "Tales of Monsters," note 20.

18. "Stepping Up."

19. We excised the conversation from this point on, since it identified Gagitlôsg' too specifically.

20. The "Trail of Tears" of 1838 still lingers in the folk-consciousness of the Western Cherokees, just as it does in that of the Eastern.

21. Cherokee, North Carolina.

22. Paint Clan—or usually so called. The etymology of the word needs some study.

23. Anisûnôi is a synonym for the nativistic secret society, the Anigituhwagi, in

which A. G. K.'s family has been very influential. Her great-uncle was the late Chief Levi Gritts of the Anigituhwagi.

24. A. G. K. is an Aniwôdi (Paint Clan).

25. The Cherokee name of James Fourkiller, Dôi's informant.

26. Most of the Eastern Cherokees speak the Middle Cherokee dialect.

27. Blue Ridge Mountains?

28. The ecology of Eastern Cherokees is exhaustively treated in GCAC.

29. The person referred to here is Dalala (N.).

30. "Cherry Tree," an Indian community a few miles south of Stilwell, Adair County.

31. AHAM, pp. 456-57.

32. Eli Smith's.

33. Asudi did not, of course, mean "summertime" in a literal sense. "Warm weather" might be a better translation.

34. Corn was the Cherokee staff of, life. A complete failure of the crop was calamitous.

35. Old "Famous."

36. The Five Civilized Tribes (Cherokees, Choctaws, Creeks, Chickasaws, and Seminoles)?

37. "The Old Stockade": Fort Smith, Arkansas.

38. This unidentified place name means "honey" or "molasses."

39. "They Are Drunk," the title of the song (and the dance).

40. The translation runs as follows:

> Ha yu wa ni ha yu wa ni ya li ha yo ya ni ha yu wa ni ya ne!
> Ha yu wa ni ga yo ya ni ga yu wa ni ga ni!
> Dilidegô says this, all night he has said it,
>   all night Dilidegô says it!
> Ya na yo ya na ho wi ya no yo ya na hi ya na wi ya na yu!
> Dilidegô says this, all night he has said it!
> Titagade says it is past midnight; he has said this!
> I also say: "Far off, he is trudging." Ya na yo!
> "He is trudging." Yo!

41. Robert Beaver.

42. The choreography of the Creeks was traditionally much esteemed by other tribes of the Southeast.

43. One of the documents in IL, a collection which is described in PBIL (p. 185), is a funeral notice which we have translated but not yet published. Written in 1871, it casts a revealing sidelight on the mortuary customs of its period.

44. There is so much in this somewhat mystical paragraph that is far from clear that we checked our translation very carefully. But this is what he said.

45. Asudi must be referring to some prophecy of pre-Removal times, for within his own lifetime the Cherokees were always divided. The allusion to a possible third segment (the Texas Cherokees) would appear to bear this out.

46. He must not have been as much in the dark as he stated: he was dressed in his Sunday best when we arrived. "I've been expecting you," he said.

47. Asudi was undoubtedly unaware of the fact that at the time of his arrival the white man was enduring the same inconveniences in making fire as was the Indian.

48. *Dawôl'* is a fungus, said to have been especially prized for fire-making when found growing in a knothole of a hickory log.

49. Fire never seems to be just fire to an old Cherokee: either it possesses sacramental qualities, or it doesn't.

50. "Bark."

51. Around Beaver Mountain, southern Adair County.

52. This statement is ambiguous in both languages. Perhaps the speaker meant: "All human yearnings to know God came from that Source."

HISTORICAL SKETCHES

1. See "Uk'ten' Stories."

2. See "Magic Is Where You Find It."

3. One wonders why it was that the Creeks, not the Cherokees, were in possession of them.

4. A prosperous and much respected citizen, now deceased, of the Itsôdiyi community. See "Ethnological Data," note 32.

5. Nel' Hayan' would be Nel', the unmarried daughter of Hayan', according to Cherokee nomenclature. Their "white" given names and patronymic would, of course, most likely be something entirely different, such as, let us say, Mary and Sally Deerinwater.

6. See "Ethnological Data," note 32.

7. The same individual referred to in "Tales of the Little People," note 14.

8. Probably from "Tobacco Pipe."

9. We cannot identify this plant.

10. Tsalagi Wil'.

11. Fort Smith. See "Ethnological Data," note 37.

12. The crime for which he was executed was the murder of Earnest Melton in Lenapah. The actual execution took place at 2:13 P.M. but preparations for it did begin at approximately the time stated by Dalala.

13. This may be one Cherokee designation for Lenapah. "Leniquoi" is also heard.

14. Bill Cook.

15. Jim Cook.

16. "Frank."

17. "Mosquito."

18. Henry Starr was the husband of the even more notorious Belle Starr. He was a Cherokee; she was white.

19. In an unrecorded conversation the narrator explained that he, his father, and his brother had been charged with the murder of a white man. All were eventually exonerated.

20. The meaning of this proper name is unknown to us.

21. Barber Store, now on Oklahoma State Highway 100, used to be some distance south of where it is now.

22. A Cherokee Baptist Church, about three miles south of Barber.

23. "One-Who-Hides Bearpaw."

24. Dry Creek.

25. "Belted Across the Rump," a hill.

26. See "Tales of the Little People," note 3.

27. "Largest Cedar Tree—Place." This Illinois River fishing hole would appear to be now submerged under Tenkiller Lake.

28. The outlaws are described as being old men, yet Cherokee Bill was but twenty years of age when he was hanged!

29. "Place of the Diamondback Rattlesnakes."

30. For some reason Asudi pronounced the name Sequoyah in the English manner, here and following.

31. The accepted date of Sequoyah's death is August, 1843. (See GFS, p. 71.)

32. There is no logical accounting for this astonishing statement by a man of habitual painful accuracy.

33. Asudi was born about 1869. In childhood or youth his father could indeed have known Sequoyah.

34. Asa Lookingglass.

35. Without hesitancy the Cherokees admit that their greatest political leader, John Ross, was but one-eighth Cherokee; but they insist that Sequoyah was a full blood, all the literature to the contrary notwithstanding. (See GFS, pp. 57-77.)

36. The literature is contradictory upon this point.

37. The literature ascribes Shawnee as well as white blood to Sequoyah.

38. This was his semi-official name in English.

39. Sequoyah's own spelling of his name, and in fact the generally accepted spelling of his name in the syllabary, is Siquôya, possibly a concession to the English manner of pronunciation (see OLPM, p. 220). Cherokees frequently pronounce it Siquôyi. Attempts to arrive at an etymology of the name without a knowledge of the language have led to some preposterous conclusions. It does not mean "He Guessed It," one of the most widely accepted "translations," nor does it mean "Pig in a Pen." The latter would be "Siqua aya." In fact, it does not mean anything, for it is not of Cherokee origin. It was undoubtedly borrowed from some other Indian language, possibly the extinct Taskigi (see the comments of Asudi, later).

40. A.G.K. was referring here to descendants.

41. A., misunderstanding, most probably thought that the questions had to do with siblings.

42. It is almost universally accepted that Sequoyah was born in Tuskegee (Tasgigi) in Tennessee and that he emigrated to what is now Arkansas in 1818 and subsequently moved to "the other side of Ekûn'," now the site of the Sequoyah Shrine.

43. Akins, in Sequoyah County.

44. For information on Sequoyah's wives and children, see SEHC, pp. 50-52.

45. Pronounced in Cherokee fashion.

46. All accounts agree that he was lame.

47. Asudi had no intention of permitting books to interrupt his train of thought upon Sequoyah.

48. The much-told account of Sequoyah's westward journey in 1842 in search of a splinter group of his people is dealt with in GFS, pp. 48-71. An official delegation sent by the Cherokee Nation in the spring of 1845 to discover Sequoyah's fate brought back a report of his death in Mexico. A few years ago the Cherokee Foundation, in a sense the heir to the legally defunct Cherokee Nation, sent an expedition to recover his remains. The senior author viewed a motion picture and conversed with Frank Muskrat, a Cherokee Foundation official and expedition member, concerning the inconclusive results of the operation.

49. We wonder why the apocryphal tradition of Sequoyah's return and burial at home, widely believed, has never passed into print before now.

50. Sallisaw, the county seat of Sequoyah County.

51. Jesse.

52. Could he have mean: Hanson?

53. "Where He Died," a Cherokee community near Nicut.

54. "Bottle Star."

55. "Smaller Ones."

56. "Dirt Thrower."

LITERATURE CITED

AHAM ADAIR, JAMES
      1775. The History of the American Indians. London. New ed., Watauga Press, 1930.

BTSM BOAS, FRANZ
      1916. Tsimshian Mythology. Bur. Amer. Ethnol. Ann. Rpt.

BUIB BRITTON, WILEY
      1922. The Union Indian Brigade in the Civil War. Franklin Hudson Pub. Co., Kansas City, Mo.

BCBL BUSHNELL, DAVID I., JR.
      1909. The Choctaw of Bayou Lacomb, St. Tammany Parish, Louisiana. Bur. Amer. Ethnol. Bull. 48.

DSSA DENSMORE, FRANCIS
      1943. A Search for Songs Among the Chitimacha Indians in Louisiana. Bur. Amer. Ethnol. Bull. 133, Anthrop. Papers 19.

DFSM 1956. Seminole Music. Bur. Amer. Ethnol. Bull. 161.

DSOB DORSEY, JAMES OWEN and SWANTON, JOHN R.
      1912. A Dictionary of the Biloxi and Ofo Languages. Bur. Amer. Ethnol. Bull. 47.

FGSC FENTON, WILLIAM N. and GULICK, JOHN (eds.)
      1961. Symposium on Cherokee and Iroquois Culture. Bur. Amer. Ethnol. Bull. 180.

GFS FOREMAN, GRANT
      1938. Sequoyah. U. of Okla. Press, Norman, Okla.

GTEC GILBERT, WILLIAM H., JR.
      1943. The Eastern Cherokees. Bur. Amer. Ethnol. Bull. 133, Anthrop. Papers 23.

GCNC 1957. The Cherokees of North Carolina: Living

Memorials of the Past. Rpt. Smith. Inst., pp. 529-55.

GCAC   GULICK, JOHN

1960. Cherokees at the Crossroads. Inst. for Research in Soc. Sci., U. of N. C., Chapel Hill, N. C.

HCBO   HARMAN, S. W.

1954. Cherokee Bill the Oklahoma Outlaw. Frontier Press of Texas, Houston, Tex.

HHAI   HODGE, FREDERICK W. (ed.)

1906. Handbook of American Indians North of Mexico. Bur. Amer. Ethnol. Bull. 30, vol. 1, 2.

HACF   HOWARD, JAMES

1959. Altamaha Cherokee Folklore and Culture. Journ. Amer. Folklore, Ap.-Je., pp. 134-38.

HMAM   HURSTON, ZORA NEALE

1935. Mules and Men. J. B. Lippincott, Philadelphia.

IL   INOLI

1848-1882. Inoli Letters (ms. coll. in Sequoyah syllabary). Archives Bur. Amer. Ethnol.

KLOC   KATE, HERMAN F. C. TEN

1899. Legends of the Cherokees. Journ. Amer. Folklore, Oct.-Dec., pp. 413-22.

MMOC (1888)   MOONEY, JAMES

1888. Myths of the Cherokees. Journ. Amer. Folklore, Ap.-Je., pp. 97-108.

MCIP

1889. Cherokee and Iroquois Parallels. Journ. Amer. Folklore, p. 67.

MSFC

1891. The Sacred Formulas of the Cherokees. Bur. Amer. Ethnol., Ann. Rpt., pp. 307-97.

MMOC

1900. Myths of the Cherokees. Bur. Amer. Ethnol., Ann. Rpt., pt. 1.

OMSM   OLBRECHTS, FRANS M. and MOONEY, JAMES

1932. The Swimmer Manuscript. Cherokee Sacred Formulas and Medicinal Prescriptions. Bur. Amer. Ethnol. Bull. 99.

OLPM   OO-NO-LEH
         1845. Letter in Sequoyah Syllabary. Reproduced in
         The American Heritage Book of Indians, American
         Heritage Pub. Co. (n.p.)

OTBB   OWL, WILLIAM
         1910. The Beautiful Bird, in The Red Man, vol.
         3, no. 3, pp. 131-32, The Carlyle Indian Press,
         Carlyle, Pa.

PBIL   PILLING, JAMES C.
         1888. Bibliography of the Iroquoian Languages. Bur.
         Amer. Ethnol. Bull. 6.

SCIT   SPECK, FRANK G.
         1907. The Creek Indians of Tasgigi Town. Mem.
         Amer. Anthrop. Assn., vol. 2, pt. 2.

SEYI   1909. Ethnology of the Yuchi Indians. Publs. Univ.
         Mus., U. of Pa., vol. 1, no. 1.

SEHC   STARR, EMMET
         1917. Early History of the Cherokees (n.p.).

SMTS   SWANTON, JOHN R.
         1929. Myths and Tales of the Southeastern Indians.
         Bur. Amer. Ethnol. Bull. 88.

SITN   1952. The Indian Tribes of North America. Bur.
         Amer. Ethnol. Bull. 145.

TDOC   TERRELL, JAMES W.
         1892. The Demon of Consumption. A Legend of
         the Cherokees in North Carolina. Journ. Amer. Folk-
         lore. Ap.-Je., pp. 125-26.

TMIF   THOMPSON, STITH
         1957. Motif-Index of Folk-Literature, vol. 4. Indi-
         ana U. Press, Bloomington, Ind.

WCHI   WITTHOFT, JOHN and HADLOCK, WENDELL S.
         1946. Cherokee-Iroquois Little People. Journ. Amer.
         Folklore, Oct.-Dec., pp. 413-22.